Quebec
and Section 33

Why the Notwithstanding
Clause Must Not Stand

Michael B. Davie

Manor House Publishing Inc.

Canadian Cataloguing in Publication Data:

Davie, Michael B.
Quebec and Section 33:
Why the Notwithstanding Clause Must Not Stand

Includes bibliographical references and notes.
ISBN: 978-0-9685803-2-5

1. Canada. Canadian Charter of Rights and Freedoms.
2. Civil rights - Canada
3. Constitutional law - Canada.
4. Constitutional history - Canada.
5. Quebec (Province) - History, Autonomy
6. Decentralization in government - Canada.
I. Title.

KE4381.D39 2000   342.71'085   C00-901620-1

Published October 15, 2000
by Manor House Publishing: **(905) 648-2193**
Printed in Canada by Friesens Corporation.
First Edition.

Great Books by Michael B. Davie

Canada Decentralized MH
Can our Nation Survive?

Quebec and Section 33 MH
Why the Notwithstanding Clause must not Stand

Inside the Witches' Coven MH
Exploring Wiccan Rituals

Enterprise 2000 MH
Hamilton, Halton and Niagara Embrace the New
Millennium

Success Stories BR
Business Achievement in Greater Hamilton and
Beyond

Hamilton: It's Happening* BR
Celebrating Hamilton's Sesquicentennial

MH = Published by Manor House Publishing. BR = Published
by BRaSH Publishing
   * = With co-author Sherry Sleightholm

Belated Credit for Past Work:

Please note: Regarding the book Enterprise 2000: Greater Hamilton, Halton and Niagara embrace the New Millennium, author Michael B. Davie should have received credit for the concept and design of the book's striking cover.

The cover depicted a limitless horizon with, in the foreground, a New Year's baby seated at a computer with the image repeated endlessly on the computer screen.

Davie also originated the back cover concept of the author leaning on the computer monitor showing the baby image, again repeated endlessly.

Photographer Paul Sparrow should have received credit for bringing these images to realization through his skilful photographic and computer montage work. These works by both gentlemen are hereby recognized.

– Manor House Publishing Inc.

For

Philippa

Acknowledgements

This book would not have been possible without the teachings and insights offered by political scientists much more learned than I. I am indebted to my talented and patient professors of political science at McMaster University. I am also thankful for the understanding of my wife Philippa and our children while I pursued a university education late in life.

- Michael B. Davie.

About the author

Michael B. Davie is an award-winning writer previously wrote *Enterprise 2000* and *Success Stories.* He also wrote over 100 business profiles and some chapter text as co-author of *Hamilton: It's Happening,* commemorating Hamilton's 150th anniversary.

Michael B. Davie is also an editor and writer with The Toronto Star, Canada's largest-circulation newspaper reaching millions of Canadian readers daily.

He's won dozens of awards for outstanding journalism and is a prolific freelance writer who reaches an international audience.

In addition to publications in the United States and Europe, his work has appeared with and without bylines in many major Canadian publications, including the Halifax Chronicle-Herald, Montreal Gazette, Winnipeg Free Press, Edmonton Journal, Calgary Herald and Vancouver Sun.

Prior to The Star, he was an editor with The Globe and Mail, Canada's national newspaper with coast-to-coast-to-coast readership.

Previous to The Globe, he spent 17 years as a reporter editor and columnist with The Hamilton Spectator, a big regional daily, where he won 28 journalism awards.

Prior to joining The Spectator, the author spent five years with other publications, including The Welland Tribune, a mid-sized daily where he provided business and political coverage as a reporter, columnist and editor.

Before The Tribune, he served two years as regional news editor for one of Ontario's largest chains of community newspapers.

His interest in writing began in childhood and as a teenage in the late 1960s to early 1970s his work began appearing in small, high school and counter-culture publications.

He turned professional in the mid-1970s as Editor of The Phoenix serving Mohawk College of Applied Arts & Technology where he earned a Broadcast Journalism diploma.

He also holds a Niagara College Print Journalism diploma and degrees in Political Science from McMaster University where he was repeatedly named to the Deans' Honour List and won the Political Science Prize for outstanding academic achievement.

His journalism awards include several Western Ontario Newspapers Association awards for exemplary business writing. He earned his most recent WONA Business Writing award in 1997. The same year, he received, in Vancouver, a national Lifetime Achievement Award for journalism.

Born and raised in Hamilton, he currently resides in Ancaster with his wife Philippa and their children Donovan, Sarah and Ryan.

CONTENTS:

Manor House Publishing Inc.
(906) 648-2193.

Introduction

The threat of Quebec separation along with that province's sign law violation of the human right of freedom of expression, and a decentralization trend that has weakened our federal government, together constitute three resilient problems for those Canadians who desire a strong central government in a united country which fully respects human rights and the freedoms normally associated with a free country.

This book will argue that these problems are worsened by Section 33 of the Canadian Charter of Rights and Freedoms which is entrenched under Schedule B of the Constitution Act, 1982.

Section 33 allows that Parliament or a provincial legislature "may expressly declare in an Act of Parliament or of the legislature, as the case may be, that the Act or a provision thereof shall operate notwithstanding a provision included in section 2 or sections 7 to 15 of this Charter."   1.

Section 33 has the effect of allowing a federal or provincial government to override section 2 establishing and protecting the existence of such fundamental freedoms as freedom of conscience and religion, freedom of thought, belief, opinion and expression, including freedom of the press and other media of communication; freedom of peaceful assembly; and freedom of association."   2.

In also allowing sections 7 to 15 to be overridden, section 33 permits governments to violate legal rights to life, liberty and security of the person, the right to be protected from unreasonable search and seizure, the right not to be arbitrarily detained or imprisoned, the right to retain counsel without delay, fair treatment rights for accused persons, the right not to be subjected to cruel and unusual punishment, plus equality rights establishing the equality of individuals under law.   3.

Any invocation of section 33 is subject to review - but only after five years, leaving the violation of rights to continue to years, outliving the government which invoked the clause.

••

1.   Constitution Act 1982, Part One, The Canadian Charter of Rights and Freedoms, section 33.
2.   Ibid, section 2.
3.   Ibid, sections 7-15.

Section 33, as Charter framer Pierre Trudeau recalls, is meant to be used rarely, "only in the most extreme and compelling circumstances," and after public debate into why a legislature is violating rights.   4.

Yet in practice, Quebec casually invoked a blanket application of the clause with little debate.

That fundamental rights and freedoms can be so easily toyed with by government is disturbing.   Jennifer Smith notes, section 33's "very appearance in the context of the Charter strikes an incongruous note and is testimony to the strength of the lingering tradition of parliamentary supremacy."   5.

Also known as the notwithstanding clause and the non obstante clause, section 33, in the view of this paper, has enhanced provincial power at the expense of the federal government, has diminished the protection of freedoms meant to be enjoyed by all Canadians and has aided divisiveness and separatism by giving Quebec a tool with which it can overrule the highest courts in our land to violate human rights.

....

4.   Pierre Trudeau Towards A Just Society, Toronto: Penguin Books, 1992, pp. 349-351.
5.   Jennifer Smith, 'The origins of judicial review in Canada', in Law, Politics and the Judicial Process in Canada, edited by F. L. Morton, Calgary: University of Calgary Press, 1992, p. 357.

The ways in which Section 33 can be so blamed, the trend of decentralization, Quebec separatism and the threat to rights will all be explored further throughout this book.

Canadians, much like the citizens of the United States and other democratic nations, enjoy fundamental freedoms of expression, of thought, of assembly, of religion and of association.

These freedoms are subject to reasonable limitations in democratic states and in Canada, this matter is clearly addressed in the Charter's judicial override, section 1, which guarantees our fundamental rights "subject only to such reasonable limits prescribed by law as can be demonstrably justified in a free and democratic society." 6.

The need for demonstrably-justified limitations on freedoms is obvious. For example, a democratic society's desire to provide protection from libel and slander naturally leads to the imposition of reasonable limits on freedom of expression.

However, the Charter's description of the fundamental rights and freedoms of Canadians as being fundamental denotes these rights as being

....

6. Constitution Act 1982, Part One, The Canadian Charter of Rights and Freedoms, Section 1.

core to citizenry and, beyond reasonable limitations, not to be tampered with by government.

As Janet Ajzenstat has stated, "it is perhaps the finest thing about liberal democracy that it guarantees negative rights, limiting the power of democratic majorities to pass laws regulating free speech, and treating citizens unequally."   7.

Yet, the use of section 33 undermines the Charter's ability to guarantee of negative rights. The fundamental freedoms of Canadians are always at risk of government tampering - however unreasonable or unfair - as the override clause allows legislatures to violate rights and freedoms "notwithstanding a provision included in section 2 or sections 7 to 15 of this Charter."   8.

Indeed, the Charter's ability to fully protect the rights and freedoms of Canadians has been seriously eroded by section 33 allowing legislatures intent on violating our rights to overrule the highest court in the land to achieve that end.

This does not render the Charter worthless as it

....

7.   Janet Ajzenstat, 'A Social Charter Eh? Thanks, But No Thanks', Hamilton: McMaster University Political Science essay,   1994, p. 3.

8.   Constitution Act 1982, Part One, The Canadian Charter of Rights and Freedoms, Section 33.

continues to provide constitutionally-entrenched protection of rights.

Rather, Section 33 imposes the constant threat that a government can, with few limitations, infringe a fundamental freedom in a manner which is not demonstrably justified in a free and democratic society (otherwise, a government would rely on meeting the test of section 1 without ever resorting to use of section 33).

Section 33 hands governments something of a loaded gun - without asking them to account for its use.

Given that government terms seldom last a full five years, it is unlikely that any given government, even if it invoked section 33 at the very start of its term, would ever be subjected to the five-year justification proviso.

The rights violation and the issue of section 33 usage would therefore become a matter for a subsequent government to deal with.

Elections are also an imperfect way of adding a measure of accountability to section 33 usage as electoral results are seldom, if ever, a decisive response to a single issue.
Override use would simply become one of many issues in debate and could well be overshadowed by economic issues.

Thus, in practical terms, governments invoking section 33 automatically win, without having to justify use of the notwithstanding clause, without having to justify a violation of fundamental freedoms.

Section 33's supporters are prone to downplay the dangers of giving legislatures the last word on violating freedoms and rights.

They note that Supreme Court of Canada Chief Justice Lyman Duff has linked responsible, executive-dominated parliamentary government with rights protection and that the British North America Act conveyed to Canada an array of civil rights and the House of Commons is a representative body, accountable to a rights-bearing electorate.   9.

This issue will be explored more fully later in this book. For now, let me state that I agree that the House should act as a rights-protecting, representative body and does much of the time.

However, I must argue that the representative quality of Parliament has been diminished by party discipline which effectively limits the ability of members to represent their constituents' views.

....

9.   Reference Re Alberta Statutes, In the Supreme Court of Canada, (1938) 2 S.C.R. 100, in: Peter H. Russell, Rainer Knopff and Ted Morton, Federalism and the Charter, Ottawa: Carleton University Press, 1993. pp. 291-298.

Unlike the U.S. where aptly-named representatives cross party lines to truly represent their constituents on issues of importance, Canada's MPs tend to toe the party line which usually means toeing the cabinet's line. Thus, the will of cabinet, a small political elite, takes precedence over that of Canadian constituents.

Canadians live under a unique federal political system in which cabinet-centred majority governments, at federal and provincial levels, are able to exercise enormous power by invoking party discipline and ramming through sweeping changes, which, under the Trudeau government included wage and price controls and the National Energy Program.

This degree of power is all the more impressive - and unsettling - when it's recalled that our first-past-the-post electoral system can deliver a majority government to the party which only obtains more votes than its competitors, not necessarily a majority of votes.

In the 1988 federal election, the Tories won a large majority of seats even though a majority of Canadians voted for other parties.

Yet, in a three party system, the Progressive Conservatives captured more votes than either rival party, returned to office with a large majority of seats and declared a mandate to negotiate a free trade agreement with the United States. Aided by party discipline, the Brian Mulroney government then gave short shrift to concerns over loss of Canadian sovereignty and quickly approved the trade pact which underwent a far more arduous approval process in the United States.

It is the view of this paper that Canada's federal and provincial legislatures are not as representative of, or accountable to, constituents as they should be - especially when contrasted with the high degree of representation found in the U.S. - and it is therefore a mistake to confer on powerful cabinets the added power of being able to override the highest courts in the land by invoking Section 33.

Although it is the legislature which ostensibly invokes the override, the reality is that the real decision is made by cabinet, either at the federal or provincial level, and the members simply fall in line under party discipline.

With a majority government in the House of Commons, debate on many bills is an almost meaningless exercise: The Opposition parties play their expected role and argue against a government bill they know will be passed. The government whip calls on the government MPs to fall in line and to no-one's surprise, the bill is made law.

Providing something of a people's check on government, the Canadian Charter of Rights and Freedoms was, from the moment of its arrival in

1982, warmly welcomed by Canadians who saw in this document the comforting cataloguing and entrenchment of the various rights and freedoms associated with the free and democratic society we live in.

Here at last was a powerful, constitutionally-entrenched charter protecting our rights and freedoms from the sweeping powers of cabinet-centred majority governments which freely used party discipline to impose their will on parliament.

Yet, as pointed out, Section 33 has succeeded in giving an already-powerful government the last word on rights infringement.

Let me also suggest that concerns over the potential abuse of Section 33 have proven well-founded. Quebec has demonstrated an unfortunate tendency to violate human rights while advancing an agenda pursuing 'sovereignty' for Quebecers who, like all Canadians, already enjoy sovereignty at federal and provincial levels of government.

The inherent threat in Section 33, described earlier in this paper, has been acted on by Quebec which violated freedom of expression through its oppressive sign law.

Quebec also invoked a blanket application of Section 33 on an array of laws, a move amounting to a pre-emptive strike against anyone who might otherwise challenge these laws. The rights of citizens should not so easily be subordinated to the whims of government. Quebec's sweeping and pre-emptory application of section 33 also contravened the intent of Charter framers Trudeau and justice minister Jean Chretien, that the override be used rarely, after debate, to correct absurd judicial decisions.   10.

Quebec's use of the override is an insult to anyone who views government as a tool of the people and not the reverse.

In addressing the practical consequences of Section 33, this book will therefore examine what can be described as the 'Quebec Problem' and its impact on rights of Canadians who reside in Quebec.

Throughout Canadian constitutional history there has been a tendency for our governing elites to short-change individual Canadians on matters of entrenched rights and freedoms, including democratic rights which are among our most cherished freedoms of expression allowing individual citizens to utilize the vote and the political process to indicate their political preferences, ideologies and desire for change.

An early example of this is the lengthy delay Canadians experienced from a British governing elite when it came to providing Upper and Lower Canadi

....

10.   Christopher P. Manfredi, Judicial Power and the Charter, Toronto: McClelland & Stewart Inc., 1993, pp. 200-201.

ans with responsible government. It took a groundswell of public pressure and outright rebellions to force some movement in the direction of more political power-representation for individuals and less for non-elected elites in early Canadian society.

Although the 1837-1838 rebellions were put down, they succeeded in convincing Britain of the need for change and this was eventually followed by greater colonial self-government and governors who were required to abide by the will of elected representatives, in short, responsible government.   11.

Significantly, the British still managed to impose the 1840 union of the Canadas against the express wishes of Lower (renamed Eastern) Canadians, and delayed fully implementing responsible government until 1847, with Confederation a further 20 years away.   12.

Governing elites have historically demonstrated a bias against reining in their own power to give priority to individual rights.

A recent manifestation of this bias is Section 33 which essentially erodes the pre-eminence of individual rights by giving cabinet elites the ability to invade this domain at will and violate rights and

11.   Douglas Francis, et. all, Origins, Toronto: Holt, Rinehart and Winston, 1988. pp. 231-232.
12.   Ibid.

freedoms. Particular attention will be paid to the history of the political process leading up to the arrival of the 1982 Charter, with examination of the federal-provincial power struggles and compromises struck by the federal government to constitutionally entrench the Charter.

It was with considerable reluctance that the federal government agreed to Section 33 in an effort to win provincial support for the Charter.

This book will conclude by advocating the outright elimination of Section 33. Or, failing that, substantial ammendments which would restrict use of the notwithstanding clause to the federal government (which has shown much less tendency to violate human rights).

The suggested ammendments to Section 33 should, taken together, have the effect of limiting the ability of legislatures to violate rights, while at the same time retaining a degree of legislative supremacy.

However, the preferred option, in the view of this paper, remains the outright elimination of the section 33 override clause.

Legislatures are able to exercise enough supremacy over the economy, natural resources, social programs, taxation, cultural programs and a myriad of measures affecting our lives without needing special powers to violate freedoms which are called fundamental in this country and are actually treated as fundamental in most enlightened, modern democratic nations.

Beyond reasonable limitations that are demonstrably justified in a free and democratic society, our rights should not be tampered with.

Our politicians are not being paid to deny us our basic human rights. Government exists to serve us - not the reverse.

This hands-off message concerning rights is all the more important given Quebec's determination to violate the rights of Canadians who happen to reside in that province.

That issue will be dealt with more fully in the following chapters, beginning with our next chapter on the Charter's evolution.

2

THE CHARTER EVOLUTION

"The government of Canada surrendered a notwithstanding clause in 1981-1982, which said, in effect, 'we hereby guarantee Canadians their fundamental rights to language, to religion and to association, but, by the way, we forgot to tell you, these fundamental rights can be overridden if the Premier of Prince Edward Island or Saskatchewan or Quebec decides it's in his interest to take them away.'"

- Brian Mulroney, Parliamentary Debates, 6 April, 1989.

Prime Minister Mulroney decried section 33 for holding rights "hostage," and denounced the clause as "that major flaw of 1981, which reduces your individual rights and mine." 12.

To gain an understanding of how section 33 has undermined the our rights and freedoms some reflection on the evolution of the Charter is a useful exercise. The Constitution Act of 1867 set out federal and provincial powers. But as George Stanley notes, it lacked the U.S. Constitution's emphasis on individual freedom and did not contain a charter of rights. 13.

Not that Canadians were without rights and freedoms prior to the Bill of Rights. Canadians relied on a combination of judicial precedents, statute laws, common laws and conventions which in sum amounted to an unwritten Charter based on centuries of international jurisprudence. 14.

As Ronald Cheffins and Patricia Johnson note, Canada has "a tradition of individual freedom without the necessity of an entrenched Charter of Rights... the starting point of our legal system is that an individual is free except to the extent restrained by law." 15.

....

12.   Brian Mulroney, House of Commons Debates, April 6, 1989, Hansard, p. 153.
13.   G. Stanley, A Short History of The Canadian Constitution, Ryerson Press, 1969. pp. 111-126.
14.   R. I. Cheffins & P. A. Johnson, The Revised Canadian Constitution. Politics As Law,   Toronto: McGraw-Hill Ryerson Limited, 1986, p. 132.
15.   Ibid., p. 69

The implied bill of rights was recognized by Supreme Court Justice Duff who struck down the Alberta Press Bil, which had censored media criticism of the government on grounds that it was ultra vires or outside the province's jurisdiction.

In his decision, the judge noted that Canadians hold implied rights of freedom of speech and press and that free and open public expression and discussion are core to truly representative parliamentary institutions, a position that has become known as the 'Duff Doctrine'. 16.

Certainly Duff is correct in establishing the way things ought to be.
Our parliaments, federal and provincial, ought to allow public expression with such reasonable limits as libel and slander laws dictate.

It is also correct to point out that Duff's views were expressed almost half a century before the existence of section 33, a time when a court ruling relating to rights could not be casually overridden by a provincial legislature.

....

16. Reference re Alberta Statutes, In the Supreme Court of Canada, 1938, 2 S.C.R. 100, in Bayard Reesor, The Canadian Constitution in Historical Perspective, Scarborough: Prentice-Hall Canada Inc., 1992, p 121.

While the negative rights contained in the Charter diminish overall the principal of legislative supremacy, section 33 goes too far towards restoring parliamentary supremacy over fundamental rights and freedoms of Canadians.

Section 33 empowered the province of Quebec to overrule the highest court in the land to violate freedom of expression and penalize Canadians for advertising in the official language of their choice.

Prior to the arrival of section 33, the effectiveness of the 'unwritten charter' had been evident in countering a number of discriminatory acts invoked by Quebec Premier Maurice Duplessis, including his Padlock Law allowing police to lock distributors of Communist literature out of their own homes.

The Supreme Court, notes Ian Greene, "did succeed to some extent in protecting civil liberties during the infamous Duplessis era."   17.

The unwritten charter, with its stare decisis use of precedents, provided courts with an effective tool for protecting rights from government tampering. Alan Cairns notes that rights were also protected by "a

....

17.   Ian Greene, The Charter of Rights, Toronto: James Lorimer & Company, Publishers, 1989, p. 21.

host of international conventions, covenants, resolutions, and treaties..." 18.

Despite this degree of rights protection success of the 'unwritten charter' however, Canadians felt the need for a set of clearly-stated and entrenched rights and freedoms as secure as possible from tampering by government.

Roy Romanow, John Whyte and Howard Leeson note that public demand led to legislation in the 1940s. . In 1944, Ontario brought in its symbolically important Racial Discrimination Act and in 1947 the CCF government of Saskatchewan enacted its Bill of Rights which not only safeguarded against racial discrimination but also protected civil liberties. 19.

This did not alter the tendency for provinces to violate rights more frequently than the federal government, but it did speak to the responsiveness of provinces to public demand for formalized rights and a desire to try to live up to formal standards. F. L. Morton, Peter Russell and Michael Whithey observe

....

18.   Alan C. Cairns, Charter Versus Federalism. The Dilemmas of Constitutional Reform, Montreal: McGill-Queen's University Press, 1992, p. 25.
19.   Roy Romanow, John Whyte, and Howard Leeson, Canada Notwithstanding, Agincourt: Carswell/Methuen, 1984. pp. 222-223.

that courts throughout North America have had to use judicial review to "restrain what is perceived as 'aberrant' behavior of regional majorities." 20.

Romanow, Whyte and Leeson note federal-provincial constitutional discussions have shifted away from jurisdictional questions to begin "a movement towards examining the position of individuals in the state."

They add that "protection of individual rights, including language rights, has begun to replace argument over respective political responsibility for legislative matters bearing on rights and language." 21.

It should be noted here that the bills of rights of Saskatchewan and other provinces also contained a notwithstanding clause.

However, this was little cause for concern as the fact that these various bills of rights were statutes meant that they could be easily amended or struck down by a legislature.

The major difference with section 33 of the Charter is that can be used to override rights that are constitutionally entrenched. These rights were deliber

....

20. F. L. Morton, Peter Russell and Michael J. Whithey, 'The First 100 Charter Decisions', in Law, Politics and the Judicial Process in Canada, edited by F. L. Morton, Calgary: University of Calgary Press, 1992, 419.

21. Roy Romanow, John Whyte, and Howard Leeson, Canada Notwithstanding., Agincourt: 1984. pp. xvi-xvii.

ately so entrenched to prevent governments from tampering with them. Yet section 33 allows governments to do just that.

In 1960, Prime Minister John Diefenbaker introduced the Canadian Bill of Rights, which also had an unnecessary override (the bill was also an easily amended statute). Diefenbaker had sought a bill of rights since the late 1940s in response to public demand for formalized rights.   22.

However, the Bill of Rights, confined matters of federal jurisdiction, was an ordinary statute, not a constitutional document, and that left judges reluctant to use it to invalidate federal legislation.   23.

The lack of constitutional entrenchment put the Bill of Rights' usefulness in doubt. Morton notes:
"From the start, the Bill of Rights was swamped by problems of interpretation. These problems stemmed principally from its legal status as an ordinary statute and the ambiguous wording of its second section. Canadian judges, including ... the Supreme Court, could not agree on what function the Bill assigned the courts."   24.

....

22.   G. Stanley, A Short History of The Canadian Constitution, 1969. pp. 163-164.
23.   Rainer Knopff and F. L. Morton, Charter Politics, Scarborough: Nelson Canada, 1992. p.19.
24.   F. L. Morton, Law, Politics and Judicial Process in Canada, edited by F. L. Morton, Calgary: University of Calgary Press, 1992. p. 398.

So reluctant were judges to rely on the Bill of Rights, that the statute was successfully used only once in the 1970 Drybones case in which the Supreme Court found that Section 94 (B) of the Indian Act violated the Indian Drybones of the right to equality before the law as the punishment given him for public intoxication was more severe than a non-native person would be accorded.

In many ways, the Bill of Rights simply fell short of providing any meaningful protection of rights. As Patrick Monahan notes, "the judicial legacy under the Bill was one of endless logical and legal posturing, apparently designed to ensure that the statute's only application would be to laws dealing with the drunkenness of Indians off their reserves in the North West Territories." 25.

The relevance of the Bill of Rights beyond its place in the evolution of formalized rights is that its shortcomings illustrated the need for a constitution-ally-entrenched charter.

As George Stanley observes, this weak bill "led to the demand for more effective protection for civil rights and for the enactment of a charter of rights

....

25.   Patrick Monahan, 'Politics and Constitutional Interpreta-tion', from Crosscurrent, Contemporary Political Issues, edited by Mark Charlton and Paul Barker, Scarborough: Nelson Canada, 1991. p. 86.

which might, like the American Bill of Rights, become an integral part of the constitution, and bind all governments, federal and provincial alike." 26.

Faced with this public demand, Pierre Trudeau, minister of justice in the Liberal government of Lester B. Pearson, introduced a draft civil rights bill incorporating freedoms of expression, conscience, religion, and association along with rights to liberty and linguistic rights. This proposed Charter of Human Rights became the subject of federal-provincial jurisdictional disputes and was referred to the 1968 Federal-Provincial Conference where it was effectively shelved. 27.

Then, three years of formal constitutional talks with the provinces ended in failure when the Victoria Charter subsequently failed to gain the support of Quebec. 28.

In 1975, Trudeau began another effort on the constitutional front with a new set of proposals which sought to address some of the division of power problems encountered in earlier efforts. This too failed and Trudeau responded in

....

26.   G. Stanley, A Short History of the Canadian Constitution, 1969. p. 165.

27.   IBID, pp. 165-166.

28.   R.D. Olling and M.W. Westmacott, The Confederation Debate: The Constitution in Crisis, Toronto: Kendall/Hunt Publishing Co., 1980, p viii.

1978 with the even more-limited Constitutional Amendment Bill C 60.

As Keith Banting and Richard Simeon note, this bill was "widely criticisized, and it suffered a mortal wound in 1979 when the Supreme Court of Canada ruled that Ottawa did not have constitutional authority to alter unilaterally the powers and membership of the Senate."   29.

Constitutional efforts took on renewed impetus with the 1980 defeat of the referendum in which the Parti Quebecois had hoped to obtain a mandate to negotiate 'sovereignty association.' but lost, bolstering the belief in Ottawa that federalism could be defended in Quebec.

As Alan Cairns notes, the defeat left Quebec and the separatists "toothless tigers in the struggle for a renewed federalism they neither believed in nor thought attainable."   30.

In campaigning against the Parti Quebecois in the referendum, Trudeau had made a promise for

....

29.   Keith Banting and Richard Simeon, And No One Cheered. Federalism, Democracy and the Constitution Act, edited by Keith Banting and Richard Simeon, Toronto: Methuen Publications, 1983. p. 4.

30.   Alan C. Cairns, 'The Politics of Constitutional Conservatism', from And No One Cheered: Federalism, Democracy and the Constitution Act, edited by Keith Banting and Richard Simeon, Toronto: Methuen Publications, 1983, p 30.

renewed federalism should his side win. It did, and Trudeau used his referendum victory as a mandate to expedite efforts to patriate the constitution and fulfil his promise to Quebec. Trudeau also threatened to act unilaterally if agreement could not be reached with the provinces.   31.

Despite the threat of unilateral action, sincere efforts got underway to negotiate a constitutional arrangement with the provinces.

Yet as Roy Romanow, John Whyte and Howard Leeson note, a series of intergovernmental meetings treated the Charter as something of an afterthought.

They note that "an irony of the constitutional talks during the summer of 1980 is that, although a charter of rights was known to be central to any package that was to be formed, and that bargaining on its terms would be intense, the ministers and officials who travelled across the country in July and August, and the first ministers who met in Ottawa in September, gave the charter remarkably little attention. During the summer the subcommittee of officials responsible for discussing the charter did not meet at all in Montreal or Toronto." 32.

....

31.   Keith Banting and Richard Simeon, And No One Cheered, Toronto, 1983, pp. 4-5.
32.   Roy Romanow, John Whyte, Howard Leeson, Canada Notwithstanding, Agincourt: Carswell/Methuen, 1984. pg. 240.

The lack of attention given the charter would come back to haunt the federal government when the provinces asserted their desire to protect, if not enhance, provincial power and the federal government reluctantly accepted Section 33 as a compromise measure to secure provincial support for the charter.

At the 1979 First Ministers' Conference, the western provinces expressed dissatisfaction with the limited extent of provincial control over natural resources.
At the same time, the Atlantic provinces sought greater control over the fisheries.

Manitoba was opposed to entrenchment of a charter of rights and the other provinces, with the exception of Ontario, wanted to confine the scope of the charter and further divide powers in favor of provinces before patriation took place.   33.

After Joe Clark and Progressive Conservatives formed a minority federal government in 1979 and lost an election months later, Trudeau and the Liberals came back with a majority government and determination to resolve the constitutional impasse.   34.

....

33.   Roy Romanow, John Whyte, Howard Leeson, Canada Notwithstanding, Agincourt: Carswell/Methuen, 1984. pg. 51.
34.   Ibid., pp. 59-62.

In September 1980, the first ministers' talks stalled over entrenchment of Charter rights, an issue of concern to the governments as it suggested a greater role for the judiciary at the expense of legislatures' expense.

Saskatchewan Premier Allan Blakeney suggested provinces could support entrenchment of rights if the charter included an override clause. Although this suggestion was not acted on then, it proved to be key to the agreement reached 14 months later. 35.

Behind the provinces' drive for a notwithstanding clause was an underlying desire to have provincial power trump the rights of individual citizens. The long-standing tendency for governing elites to shortchange Canadians on protected rights, as discussed in our introductory chapter, was alive and well in a majority of provincial governments.

David Milne notes that most provinces tried to obtain "serious changes or deletions in an attempt to gut the charter." Milne observes that "only New Brunswick, Ontario and Newfoundland even accepted the principle of an entrenched charter - the Liberal spirit of nation building was being spurned by provincial elites, while federal Liberals came to regard

....

35.   Roy Romanow, John Whyte, Howard Leeson, Canada Notwithstanding, Agincourt: 1984. p. 241-2.

regionalism and province building as 'separatism by another name.'"   36.

Milne notes that "as careful students of American constitutional developments have long recognized, a rights charter as interpreted by a pro-federal Supreme Court can declare and enforce common values and practices in an otherwise diverse federation."

Milne adds that there was "therefore more than a hint of covert war against the excesses of Quebec nationalism and regionalism in Trudeau's proposal for unified values under a charter of rights."   37.

Unfortunately, as Milne also notes, to obtain a constitutional deal, federal politicians were "ready to compromise on almost all the human rights and freedoms in the package until left with a weak charter of rights that made a mockery of the protection of civil liberties..."   38.

In exchange for accepting the entrenchment of minority language rights for their provinces, the provincial governments demanded a notwithstanding clause - the right to legislate so as to expressly over

....

36.   David Milne, The Canadian Constitution, Toronto: James Lorimer & Company Publishers, 1991, p. 70.
37.   Ibid.
38.   Ibid.

ride certain sections of the charter whenever their legislatures might think it necessary. This, as Milne concludes, "was the essential bargain struck." 39.

It should also be noted Prime Minister Pierre Trudeau and Justice Minister Jean Chretien initially rejected Saskatchewan's earliest attempts to strike a compromise deal by inserting a non obstante clause. Trudeau and Chretien felt such a clause would weaken the protection of fundamental freedoms. 40.

During a 1994 television interview, Trudeau recalled the constitutional talks and expressed regret that the compromise agreement "gutted the charter with a notwithstanding clause." 41.

Several draft charters were discussed by the first ministers and on August 22, 1980, the federal government issued a new draft with a revised Section 1 stating that rights entrenched in the charter were "subject only to such reasonable limits as are generally accepted in a free and democratic society," a phrase that is close in content to the final version of Section 1.

....

39. David Milne, The Canadian Constitution, Toronto: James Lorimer & Company, p. 168.
40. Roy Romanow, John Whyte, Howard Leeson, Canada Notwithstanding, Agincourt: 1984. p 210-11.
41. Memoirs, CBC Television, Feb. 6, 1994, 9 p.m. broadcast on Canadian television.

As Romanow, Whyte and Leeson suggest, the Section 1 limitation clause already served to limit rights and freedoms to such a degree that a non obstante clause was not necessary. They note:

"Clearly the (limitation) clause was de signed to encourage judicial deference to legisla tive choices even though they affected civil liberties. From the perspective of those who were opposed to entrenchment, the limitat ion was, in some ways, superior to a non obstante clause. Under it there was no need for an explicit legislative expression of intent to override the charter in order to benefit from the limitation." 42.

Of course, Section 1, even in draft form, did not give carte blanche to legislatures. As Romanow, Whyte and Leeson also observe:

"A court would need to be convinced that the legislation that limited the rights was, in fact, generally accepted. This standard would certainly not help a province that designed innovative social legislation which imposed burdens on civil liberties of individuals." 43.

Within a week of the federal government's July

....

42.   Roy Romanow, John Whyte, Howard Leeson, Canada Notwithstanding, Agincourt: 1984. pg. 243.
43.   Ibid., p. 243.

draft of the charter, the provinces issued a proposed charter of their own which also allowed legislatures some leeway in the field of rights,provided such incursions could be considered reasonable. Romanow, Whyte and Leeson offered this observation:

> "Given the limited nature of this docu
> ment, there was no need for it to contain a
> non obstante clause. The protection of funda
> mental freedoms in the provincial document
> was couched with a limitation clause which
> stated that the rights were subject to limits
> "as are generally accepted in a free society
> living under a parliamentary democracy." 44.

After hearing from citizens groups and individuals, the overwhelming majority of whom wanted a strong charter, the government, in October 1980 proposed a charter which would be binding on the federal and provincial governments. 45.

The Section 1 limitation clause was altered to its current wording stating that limitations need be "demonstrably justified," and that such limitations should be "prescribed by law," with both changes intended to place greater onus on government to justify an infringement of rights. 46.

....

44.   Roy Romanow, John Whyte, Howard Leeson, Canada
Notwithstanding, Agincourt: 1984. p. 244.
45.   Ibid., pp. 248-249
46.   Ibid., pp. 250-251.

The final version of Section 1 still allowed governments to encroach on rights by applying "such reasonable limits prescribed by law as can be demonstrably justified in a free and democratic society."

This judicial override would not be invoked as long as a legislature could show a limitation on rights was justified.

Should a legislature wish to limit rights in manner which is reasonable, fair and justified, the judicial override of section 1 is there to greet them with a fair and reasonable test which must be met. 47.

However, if a legislature is intent on limiting rights in a manner which is unreasonable and unjustified, section 1 will no longer suffice as it upholds legislative supremacy only to the extent that legislative limitations on rights are demonstrably justified and reasonable.

For legislatures intent on violating human rights in an unreasonable and unjustified manner, section 1 will no longer suffice and section 33 presents itself as a legalistic weapon of choice to uphold a violation of rights which would otherwise be unconstitutional.

....

47.   Roy Romanow, John Whyte, Howard Leeson, Canada Notwithstanding, Agincourt: 1984. p. 244.

As Romanow, Whyte and Leeson state:

> "The choice by ten of the governments of Canada to include in the Charter of Rights and Freedoms a provision enabling legislative bodies to override the protections of the charter has been said to destroy the very idea of entrenchment. To the extent that constitutional rights are viewed as claims which, in every instance, can prevail over the wish of legislative majorities, the charter does not provide rights, at least in respect of fundamental freedoms, legal rights, and equality rights." 48.

After noting that the charter's fundamental rights and freedoms stand - but only until they are challenged by a government invoking section 33 - Romanow, Whyte and Leeson add:

> "However, the override clause means that the values which are found in the charter may not, in every case, be saved from attack by determined majorities." 49.

The override clause became part of the 'kitchen accord' reached by the federal government and provinces other than Quebec after talks had again reached an impasses. This agreement included the non obstante clause advocated by Saskatchewan and backed

....

48. Roy Romanow, John Whyte, Howard Leeson, Canada Notwithstanding, Agincourt: 1984. p. 259.
49. Ibid, p.159

by the provinces. The federal government reluctantly agreed to this clause as a compromise to achieve agreement.   50.

Although Quebec objected to not being included in the agreement, Romanow, Whyte and Leeson note that Quebec had previously broken away from the other premiers and had never seriously considered any compromise action which might undermine its separatist agenda.

They further note that Quebec had been part of a Gang of Eight (the provinces except Ontario and New Brunswick) opposed to Ottawa's threats of unilateral action on the constitution - until Quebec broke from the gang.

Ultimately, a compromise was reached, one which did not include the separatist Quebec government, and one in which the western provinces succeeded in getting the federal government to agree to the section 33 override clause in the Canadian Charter of Rights and Freedoms.

Referring to the outcome as a "blunt and brutal compromise," Alan Cairns suggests that the federal government deliberately linked the Charter with the constitution (they could have been dealt with separately) as a means of using public popularity for the

....
50.   Roy Romanow, John Whyte, Howard Leeson, Canada Notwithstanding, Agincourt: 1984. p. 202-9.

Charter to build support and legitimacy for its constitutional efforts and threats of unilateral action. 51.

The compromise was viewed harshly in Quebec. Referring to the kitchen accord as the "day of the dupes," Gerard Bergeron said the agreement was reached "in the dark of night, in some prosaic back room," in which "three conspirators (Jean Cretien, Roy McMurtry and Roy Romanow) concluded a sort of horse traders' deal, while deliberately excluding Quebec's representatives, to save the 'last ditch attempt' to reach a consensus." 52.

Given the outrage emanating from Quebec, it may well have been politic for Trudeau to have invited Levesque to breakfast with an offer to bring him in on the deal. This at least would have given Trudeau the right to claim that Quebec was given every chance to back it. However, Trudeau was concerned the other premiers might have second thoughts and he decided to take the agreement and run.

However, as Romanow, Whyte and Leeson reasonably suggest, it was also unrealistic to expect

....
51.   Alan C. Cairns, The Politics of Constitutional Conservatism, from And No One Cheered, edited by Keith Banting and Richard Simeon, Toronto: Methuen Publications, 1983. pp. 41-55.
52.   Gerard Bergeron, 'Quebec in Isolation', from And No One Cheered, edited by Keith Banting and Richard Simeon, Toronto: 1983, p. 59.

the separatist Premier Levesque would have joined the other premiers in supporting the compromise proposal - now carrying the override clause - worked out by Ottawa and the other provinces.

They observe that Quebec had bluntly stated its refusal to consider a compromise charter "and Quebec's subsequent claims of betrayal lacked factual basis." They add that "Quebec's sole objective at this stage of the negotiations was to wreck Ottawa's plan for patriation. A defeat of the federal resolution repre- sented a 'successful' conference for Quebec."   53.

Quebec had also read far too much into Trudeau's promise of renewed federalism and has wrongly interpreted this as some sort of pledge for greater provincial autonomy. However, Trudeau had made it clear in his 'Time for Action' and other published statements preceding the talks that no one should expect greater decentralization.   54.

Furthermore, the Constitution 1982 contained the amending formula Quebec had agreed to and it ad- dressed a number of Quebec's concerns including the

....

53.   Roy Romanow, John Whyte, Howard Leeson, Canada Notwithstanding, Agincourt: 1984. p. 265.
54.   Raymond Hudon, 'Quebec, the Economy and the Constitu- tion, in And No One Cheered, edited by Keith Banting and Richard Simeon, Toronto: Methuen Publications, 1983, p. 139.

right to withdraw from ammendments which derogate from a province's existing powers, thereby guaranteeing that none of Quebec's existing legislative powers will be diminished.   55.

Levesque began spreading the message that the constitutional arrangement lacked legitimacy in Quebec.

Of course he knew that it was a legitimate arrangement that was binding on Quebec and he made early use of the constitution by applying a blanket use of the Section 33 override to an array of Quebec legislation.   56.

This casual, sweeping use of Section 33 amounted to an abuse of a provision which was meant to used carefully and sparingly on specific matters of concern to governments. Blanket use of the override amounted to a pre-emptive strike against anyone who might otherwise challenge Quebec legislation.

In December 1985, Robert Bourassa and the Liberals returned to power in Quebec and began

....

55.   Roy Romanow, John Whyte, Howard Leeson, Canada Notwithstanding, Agincourt: 1984. p. 266.
56.   Peter Russell, 'Bold Statescraft, Questionable Jurisprudence,' from And No One Cheered, edited by Keith Banting and Richard Simeon, Toronto: Methuen, 1983, p. 211.

negotiations with the federal government of Brian Mulroney and the provinces to arrive at a constitutional agreement which Quebec would feel comfortable signing.

In an extraordinary exercise of goodwill and co-operation among governments, an agreement was reached on April 30, 1987 between all 11 governments, despite the reservations of some over a clause giving Quebec an ill-defined recognition as a distinct society and an amending formula which concentrated veto powers in the hands of Quebec and Ontario.

During the next three years, the Meech Lake Accord was approved by Quebec and seven other governments, including Newfoundland.

The Meech Lake Accord began to unravel when a new Newfoundland government under Clyde Wells rescinded the approval given by the former government of Brian Peckford.

New Brunswick and Manitoba also changed governments and their new premiers had difficulty in accepting the Accord in the wake of Bourassa's decision to invoke section 33 to uphold an amended Quebec sign law (Bill 178) which still carried judicially unacceptable restrictions on the use of English language on signs.

In 1990, Mulroney called a First Ministers Conference to negotiate legislative unanimity but when the June 24, 1990 deadline arrived, Manitoba and Newfoundland assemblies had not passed the Accord and it failed.

Although Bourassa's use of section 33 regarding Bill 178 had done much to undermine the Accord and although only one provincial government actually scuttled it, Bourassa nonetheless reached the fantastic conclusion that the Accord's collapse "sent a strong message to the people of Quebec: from now on, they and they alone would have to make the necessary decisions and choices regarding their political and constitutional future." 57.

Why did Meech die? A large measure of the blame must fall on Bourassa.

In December, 1988, midway into the three-year approval period required for the Accord, the Quebec Premier reached a new low.

Bourassa threw a political bombshell into the co-operative huddle of first ministers: The Supreme Court of Canada, ruling in the Devine and Ford cases, struck down the Quebec sign law for violating freedom of expression - and Bourassa responded with Section 33.

....

57. Robert Bourassa, as quoted in Michel Belanger, Jean Campeau, et. al., Report of The Commission On The Political and Constitutional Future of Quebec, Sherbrooke: Bureau d'information a Montreal, Sherbrooke, March 1991, p. 85.

Reesor notes that Bourassa "announced his intention to override both Quebec's Charter of Human Rights and the Canadian Charter and require French-only outdoor signs and French-dominant indoor signs."   58.

The outcome of Bourassa's move, Bill 178, met with outrage and bewilderment from Canadians who had trusted the 'federalist' politician not to perpetuate the anti-English actions of his predecessor. As Bayard Reesor notes:

"The political fallout in Canada was immediate. In Quebec, Bourassa was denounced by the English minority (as one would expect), but also by the French majoritywho demanded stronger actions against the English language. Bourassa's move also had profound implications for the Meech Lake Accord. The Manitoba legislature, one of two legislatures yet to ratify the Accord, was ready to debate the Accord when Bourassa announced his intention. Manitoba Premier Filmon immediately with drew the Meech Lake resolution thereby, in retrospect, probably ensuring the Accord's death."   59.

....

58. Bayard Reesor, The Canadian Constitution in Historical Perspective, Prentice Hall Canada Inc., Scarborough: 1992. p. 305.
59. Ibid.

Although the Supreme Court's decision prompted an increase in popular support for Law 101 and for the Parti Quebecois, Morton, Russell and Whithey similarly agree that "Premier Bourassa's use of the Section 33 override to re-instate restrictions on English language advertising was widely criticized and contributed to the eventual defeat of the Meech Lake Accord."   60.

Bourassa had poisoned the co-operative spirit of Meech Lake while giving Canadians grave cause for concern over the protection of anglophone minority rights in Quebec and over Quebec's transparent attempts to seize additional powers.

This sense of distrust was exacerbated by Quebec's Allaire report and Belanger-Campeau report, which will be discussed in more detail later on, and would carry over into the Charlottetown Accord process which will be addressed next.

In sharp contrast to the closed-door Meech Lake approach, the Charlottetown approach involved input from many 'ordinary' Canadians and it quickly became apparent that many were uncomfortable with even existing degrees of asymmetrical federalism.

....

60. F. L. Morton, Peter Russell and Michael J. Whithey, 'The First 100 Charter Decisions', in Law, Politics and the Judicial Process, edited by F. L. Morton, Calgary: U of Calgary Press, 1992, p. 419.

As Russell notes, the Charlottetown Accord kept special treatment for Quebec to a minimum by extending many Quebec demands - for example opting out of federal programs provisions - to all provinces.   61.

Unfortunately, in the view of this paper, such siphoning off of powers to the provinces fueled decentralization (to be discussed more fully in its own chapter).

Under Charlottetown, section 33 usage was even extended to Aboriginal governments, an unusual decentralist move which could have allowed even non-elected bodies representing tiny communities to overrule the highest court in Canada to violate individual rights.   62.

In a legally non-binding (but politically binding) referendum, Canadians were being asked to vote on an agreement which left intact provincial access to section 33 and extended this access to undefined Aboriginal governments.

Added to concerns relating to the notwithstanding clause and a weakened Charter were others:

....

61.   Peter Russell, Constitutional Odyssey, Toronto: University of Toronto Press, 1993, pp. 197-200.
62.   Ibid., pp. 190-197.

The agreement also guaranteed Quebec 25 per cent of Commons seats for all time regardless of its future share of the Canadian population.

The same agreement also failed to define what powers might be given an elected senate.

Presumably these powers would have to be substantial since the likelihood of fewer senators than MPs would mean the average senator would represent a far larger constituency than most MPs and would therefore have earned a larger mandate.

None of this was defined. Canadians were, in effect, being asked to buy a pig in a poke.

On October 26, 1992, a majority of Canadians - including those in Quebec - voted 'no' in the referendum and the Accord died.   63.

....

63.   Peter Russell, Constitutional Odyssey, Toronto: University of Toronto Press, 1993, pp. 190-207.

"It is not credible to argue that removal of the override clause will produce a shift in the balance of power between political decision-makers and courts that will change the nature of our society. Constitutionalism already exacts a high price on the autonomy of electoral politics. Most Canadians see this as legitimate and fair in order to maintain the integrity of our national commitment to federalism....

- John D. Whyte

3

WHY NOTWITHSTANDING SHOULD NOT STAND

As we've seen from previous chapters, most of the provinces were quite willing to gut the Charter of any meaningful protection of rights and they were able, in the end, to wrest a notwithstanding clause from the government to ensure they would be able to override constitutionally-entrenched fundamental freedoms at will.

Many Canadians are unhappy that the federal government - let alone a provincial government elite - should be able to override the highest court in the country to violate our rights in a manner which cannot be demonstrably justified as a reasonable limitation. `

Milne notes that when Bourassa set aside Canadian and Quebec charters of rights and invoked section 33 expressly to overrule the Court and violate rights, he "confirmed the worst fears of critics respecting the legislative loopholes in Canadian protection for citizens."   64.

Why then, aside from province-building elitists, does section 33 have supporters?

The answer to this question rests heavily on theory and principles with much less weight given to the actual uses that have so far been made of the highly controversial section 33.

Russell acknoledges that Quebec should not have used the override in the manner it did.

But Russell asks us to look past this abuse and consider his defence that notwithstanding upholds the principle of parliamentary supremacy:

> "Judges are not infallible. They may make decisions about the limits and nature of rights and freedoms that are extremely questionable. There should be some process, more reasoned than court packing and more accessible than

64.   David Milne, The Canadian Constitution, Toronto: James Lorimer & Company Publishers, 1991, p. 231.

constitutional amendment, through which the justice and wisdom of these decisions can be publicly discussed and possibly rejected. A legislative override (Section 33 - the Notwith standing Clause) provides such a process." 65.

Russell's argument places him somewhat along-side Saskatchewan Premier Allan Blakeney who saw the Charter as transferring responsibility for rights from elected representatives to non-elected courts, while Prime Minister Pierre Trudeau took a counter-ing view of the Charter, supporting it for conferring on Canadians a set of rights which could not be abused by public authorities. 66.

However, Russell qualifies his argument, cau-tioning that in his view, the override "should not be defended on the grounds that appointed judges must never be able to thwart the will of a body elected by the majority."

He notes that such a defence would rest on "the most simplistic and illiberal conception of democracy, a conception oblivious to the need for checks and

....

65. Peter H. Russell, 'Standing Up For Notwithstanding', in F. L. Morton, Law, Politics and the Judicial Process, Calgary: University of Calgary Press, 1992, p. 476.
66. F. L. Morton, Law, Politics and the Judicial Process, Calgary: University of Calgary Press, 1992, p 356.

balances as a condition of liberty and oblivious to the injustices which a majority may wish to inflict on a minority." 67.

Russell adds that "most often we will accept the decisions of the courts on these rights issues, but occasionally situations will arise in which the citizenry through a responsible and accountable process conclude that a judicial resolution of a rights issue is seriously flawed and seek to reverse it. These are the situations in which we should enjoy the benefit of the legislative override." 68.

Let me interject here with an assertion that Russell's views sound plausible - even supportable, but on a theoretical basis.

But I cannot, in good conscience, set aside the hard realities in which section 33 has been used: It was not the Canadian citizenry in Quebec which invoked Section 33, but a cabinet-dominated provincial government, with little debate or public consultation of any kind.

Nor was the correction - Bill 178 - any reflection of what the citizens wanted (I'll expand on that in

••
67.   Peter H. Russell, 'Standing Up For Notwithstanding', in F. L. Morton, Law, Politics and the Judicial Process, Calgary: University of Calgary Press, 1992, p. 476.
68.   Ibid.

a moment). Nor was there anything flawed about the courts' rulings. Both the Quebec Court of Appeal and the Supreme Court of Canada correctly found the sign law to be a violation of human rights, an unjustified attack on freedom of expression rights in the Quebec and Canadian charters of rights and freedoms.

In the earlier blanket application of section 33, no judicial decision was being 'corrected' because the judiciary was frozen out of the process by a pre-emptive use of the override on an array of legislation.

In fairness to Russell, I must again stress that his support for section 33 is both restrained and heavily qualified.

Russell cautions that his defence of the override hinges on it being "properly used." For example, Quebec's blanket application of the override did not constitute proper usage because it was not "invoked only after a reasoned debate in the legislature."

He adds that "the primary purpose of the override is to provide an opportunity for responsible and accountable public discussion of rights issues, a purpose that may be seriously undermined if legislatures are free to use the override without discussion and deliberation."   69.

....

69.   Peter H. Russell, 'Standing Up For Notwithstanding', from   F. L. Morton, Law, Politics and the Judicial Process, Calgary: University of Calgary Press, 1992, p. 479.

Acknowledging that many people felt the over-ride should not have been used to reinstate the 'French-only' sign law and that this contributed to the failure of Meech, Russell advocates reforms to section 33 usage, including requiring legislatures to identify those legislative provisions which in its judgement need protection and identify the right or freedom affected.

Russell would also subject override use to two enactments, "one before and one after an election."

He adds that this would provide a "cooling off period and time for second thoughts," while ensuring some "broad citizen involvement, thus contributing to the fundamental value process of the override."   70.

With all the above strings attached, Russell feels section 33 is worth keeping as it would be wrong to "exclude citizens and their elected legislators from the ultimate determination of these issues."   71.

However, it must be restated that we have seen remarkably little citizen involvement - or even citizens' advance knowledge - concerning the use of section 33. The clause has been used in haste to

....

70.   Peter H. Russell, 'Standing Up For Notwithstanding', from F. L. Morton, Law, Politics and the Judicial Process, Calgary: University of Calgary Press, 1992, p. 482.
71.   Ibid., p. 480.

advance government goals which, at the very least, deserved further scrutiny.

It must also be said that in respect to the vast majority of matters - especially those not concerning fundamental rights - that go before a legislature, the legislature will remain supreme. As John Whyte notes:
"It is not credible to argue that removal of the override clause will produce a shift in the balance of power between political decision-makers and courts that will change the nature of our society. Constitutionalism already exacts a high price on the autonomy of electoral politics. Most Canadians see this as legitimate and fair in order to maintain the integrity of our national commitment to federalism. Undoubtedly the Charter of Rights has produced additional re straints on democratic politics. However, it has not made irrelevant the role of politics in shap ing the nature of our society."   72.

Indeed, legislatures have enough power over citizens. Cabinet-dominated majority governments can quickly ram through legislation - such as the Canada-United States Free Trade Agreement - with a speed and certainty absent in the U.S. where a lack of party discipline and greater accountability ensures

....

72.   John D. Whyte, 'On Not Standing for Notwithstanding', from F. L. Morton, Law, Politics and the Judicial Process, Calgary: University of Calgary Press, 1992, p. 472.

riding concerns - not just party concerns - will be fully considered.

The combination of powerful governments and section 33 is worrisome and may be dampening the enthusiasm once held for the override.

Manfredi notes that the override is now seen by some as being contrary to the premise that a liberal constitutionalism involves the presence of checks on political power. A judicial check is meaningless if the legislature can overrule it. [73].

Certainly Russell's override support is cautiously qualified. He supports it if it is properly used, if there is full debate, if there is broad citizen involvement, if it receives two enactments, if affected rights and freedoms are identified, if the legislature explains why it is being used and so on.

Patrick Monahan has gone much further than heavily-qualifying his support or entertaining second thoughts: He's dropped his support for section 33 entirely.

In 1987, Monahan was defending the override on familiar principles that it demonstrates confidence

....

73.   Christopher P. Manfredi, Judicial Power and The Charter, Toronto: McClelland & Stewart, 1993, p. 203.

in the political process and ability of legislatures while ensuring unreasonable judicial rulings can be overturned.   74.

Four years, and Meech Lake's failure, later, Monahan was openly admitting that section 33, the divisive result of raw political bargaining, is now embedded in the Charter, is driving a wedge between Quebec and the rest of Canada, and is "clearly a very serious mistake."   75.

Manfredi suggests that Bourassa's ill use of the override has, for many, forever poisoned a prior willingness to consider that it might be used in a more positive manner.

Manfredi adds that "as Patrick Monahan's conversion on the section 33 issue indicates, to suggest in the post-Bill 178 era that any use of the legislative override might be justified amounts to political heresy."   76.

....

74.   Patrick Monahan, Politics and the Constitution: The Charter, Federalism and the Supreme Court of Canada, Toronto: Carswell/Metheum, 1987, pp. 118-119.
75.   Patrick Monahan, Meech Lake: The Inside Story, Toronto: University of Toronto Press, 1991, pp. 165-169.
76.   Christopher P. Manfredi, Judicial Power and The Charter, Toronto: McClelland & Stewart, 1993, p. 205.

Andrew Heard has gone so far as to suggest that a strong, politically-binding convention is emerging in Canada, outside Quebec, never to use the override clause again.   77.

Whyte suggests the desire to abolish use of the override will grow as "the anxiety that produced the political demand for entrenched rights cannot rationally be calmed in the face of legislative power granted by Section 33."

As well, Whyte fears "political authority will, at some point, be exercised oppressively; that is, it will be exercised to impose very serious burdens on groups of people when there is no rational justification for doing so."   78.

Whyte also warns that "the more that we succeed in marginalizing section 33 by pointing to its rare use and speaking of its deployment in extraordinary circumstances only, the more the legislative override will become associated with the intense politics that produce political oppression."   79.

77.   Andrew Heard, Canadian Constitutional Conventions: The Marriage of Law and Politics, Toronto: Oxford University Press, 1991, p. 147.
78.   John D. Whyte, 'On Not Standing for Notwithstanding', from F. L. Morton, Law, Politics and the Judicial Process, Calgary: University of Calgary Press, 1992, p. 472.
79.   John D. Whyte, 'On Not Standing for Notwithstanding', from F. L. Morton, Law, Politics and the Judicial Process, U. of Calgary Press, 1992, pp. 472.

As Whyte concludes, "it seems perverse to advocate the retention of a provision which is most likely to be used to preclude judicial intervention when the process has its strongest moral claim, and when the radically dispossessed will have no route for salvation other than appealing to courts to intervene on behalf of the Charter values of liberty, equality and due process." 80.

Indeed, this writer might have a different view of section 33 if legislatures were using it to ride in on a white horse and rescue us from a rights-violating judiciary.

It is difficult to imagine a situation in which this would arise, given the structure of the override and its tilt towards allowing legislatures to override individual freedoms.

However, if we can imagine a federal government passing legislation giving all Canadians the right not to be ever exposed to excessively violent films and we can further imagine the courts striking this down as a violation of freedom of expression, we could well see support for the override. Of course the situation I've just described is unlikely.

....

80.   John D. Whyte, 'On Not Standing for Notwithstanding', from F. L. Morton, Law, Politics and the Judicial Process, Calgary: University of Calgary Press, 1992, pp. 472-473.

The reality is that it is the Court that is riding in on a white horse to save our rights - and the legislature, armed with the override is charging back on its dark horse to snatch them away. An example of such a rights infringement is Quebec's use of the override to re-instate restrictions on English language advertising, a widely-criticized move which contributed to the collapse of the Meech Lake Accord.   81.

Bourassa further galvanized the distrust of Canadians towards Quebec and Meech Lake when he asserted that the Accord would have given him all the powers he needed to violate freedom of expression without resorting to section 33, a statement Milne describes as "a presumptive declaration that the legislative branch with its defence of so-called 'collective rights' ought to prevail in conflicts with the judicial branch upholding individual rights." He adds "nothing could have been more repugnant to the emerging charter norms in English-speaking Canada."   82.

Calling Bill 178 a "disastrous blow for the Meech Lake Accord," Milne adds that "since Quebec had failed to demonstrably justify that promoting the French fact required such severe limitations on funda

....

81.   F. L. Morton, Peter Russell and Michael J. Whithey, 'The First 100 Charter Decisions', in Law, Politics and the Judicial Process, edited by F. L. Morton, Calgary: U. of Calgary Press, 1992, 419.

82.   David Milne, The Canadian Constitution, Toronto: James Lorimer & Company Publishers, 1991, p. 299.

mental freedom of expression guaranteed under the charters, such a law could stand only by defying the court with ... the now-notorious notwithstanding clause." 83.

Quebec's uses of section 33 deserve closer examination, beginning with its initial, blanket application of the override. The Quebec National Assembly passed Bill 62, on June 23, 1982, applying a blanket amendment to Quebec legislation to include the override clause. Manfredi notes Quebec's blanket use of the override contravened framers' intentions it be used sparingly against specific judicial rulings. As he adds, this meant Quebec was using the override to "make a pre-emptive strike against a document to which it had refused to give its assent." 84.

In the Ford v. A.-G. Quebec case of 1988 in which the Supreme Court of Canada struck down Quebec's French-only sign law, the court upheld the Bill 62 blanket use of the override clause which was previously ruled invalid by the Quebec Court of Appeal in the Alliance des Professeurs de Montreal v. A.-G. Quebec case in 1985 as it did not include the full text of each relevant Charter section affected. 85.

....

83.   IBID, P. 231.
84.   Christopher P. Manfredi, Judicial Power and the Charter, Toronto: McClelland & Stewart Inc., 1993, pp. 200-201.
85.   Quebec v. Ford et al., Supreme Court of Canada. Judgement, Dec. 15, 1988, in Peter H. Russell, Rainer Knopff and Ted Morton, Federalism and the Charter, Ottawa: Carleton U. Press, 1993, pp. 557-581.

Saskatchewan's 1986 use of the notwithstanding clause similarly contravened federal, if not provincial, framers' intent as that province applied the override to back-to-work legislation requiring workers to adhere to a conciliator's arbitrated contract settlement.

This application of section 33 was in advance of any judicial ruling and was an attempt to insulate from judicial review a law seen by its opponents as a violation of freedom of association. This was in essence another pre-emptive strike in advance of any judicial challenge and as Manfredi observes, it too belied federal notions that the override was to be used as a "safety valve" against judicial mistakes.   86.

The judicial decisions allowing Quebec's blanket use of section 33 and Saskatchewan's similar usage on back-to-work legislation also delivered a message that use of the override clause would not have to first meet the test of satisfying the 'reasonable' requirements of section 1 of the Charter.

Manfredi notes that the Ford decision showed that "the use of section 33 would only be subject to minimal judicial scrutiny according to narrow standards of formal procedure."   87.

....

86.   Christopher P. Manfredi, Judicial Power and the Charter, Toronto: McClelland & Stewart Inc., 1993, pp. 200-201.
87.   Christopher P. Manfredi, Judicial Power and the Charter, Toronto: McClelland & Stewart Inc., 1993, pp. 202.

The importance of the minimal scrutiny rulings was that it made it easier - and therefore more likely - for governments to use section 33 without having to account for its use under section 1.

As significant as the minimal scrutiny finding was, the primary importance of the Ford decision was that the Court struck down Bill 101, a law prohibiting the use of English on commercial signs and advertising. This law, part of Quebec's French Language Charter, had not been protected by the blanket use of the override, which lapsed in 1987, and was a clear violation of fundamental freedoms of expression held in Canadian and Quebec charters of rights.   88.

The Supreme Court had, in 1979, already overturned portions of Bill 101, which would have made French the exclusive language of Quebec's legislature and courts, as this was a violation of constitutionally entrenched language rights. The Court, in 1984, also overturned a portion of Bill 101 which would have banned Canadians moving to Quebec from enrolling in English language schools as this legislation was also a violation of constitutionally entrenched language rights.   89.

Interestingly, the overturning by the Court of

....

88.   Quebec v. Ford et al., In the Supreme Court of Canada. Judgement rendered Dec. 15, 1988., in Peter H. Russell, Rainer Knopff and Ted Morton, Federalism and the Charter, Ottawa: Carleton University Press, 1993, pp. 557-581.

89.   Peter H. Russell, Rainer Knopff and Ted Morton, Federalism and the Charter, Ottawa: Carleton University Press, 1993, pp. 557-559.

Appeal of one of the most important pieces of a separatist government's anti-English, French-only legislation came to be grudgingly accepted in Quebec.

So did the striking down of Premier Maurice Duplessis's earlier laws against Jehovah Witnesses and communists. After a bit of grumbling, many in the Quebec public took to heart the judicial message that their provincial government was out of line with its unacceptable anti-minority laws. Quebec society needed to be told that these laws were illegitimate violations of individual freedom and the courts effectively delivered that message to a public which came to accept this truth.

Indeed, as Quebec society subsequently went through the so-called Quiet Revolution in the 1960s and became more enlightened, the anti-minority laws came to be seen as embarassing evidence of a past dark age out of step with the new, more liberal society. Similarly, any public grumbling over the later striking down of unconstitutional, anti-minority pieces of Bill 101 in the late 1970s through early 1980s had subsided by the time the Court turned its attention to the sign law in 1988.

With the exception of the sign law, the cases cited above have two things in common: First, the unwarranted, illegitimate violations of rights and freedoms were rightfully denounced as such by the courts and struck down in a legally binding ruling.

Secondly, section 33 did not apply to any of these cases. Duplessis's dark age predates the Charter so this quasi-tyrant was not able to use section 33 to override court decisions and continue his tirades against innocent minorities, as he surely would have if given the opportunity. In later Bill 101 cases, the Quebec government was trying to obliterate official language rights and minority language educational rights which are protected by Charter sections 16-22 and by section 23 respectively and are not subject to the section 33 override.   90.

Unfortunately, although the sign law concerned language, this commercial usage did not fall under the protection of Charter sections 16-23 but was instead a matter of fundamental freedom of expression under section 2 and was therefore vulnerable to the section 33 override.   91.

Let me suggest here that were it not for the existence of section 33, there is a reasonable chance that the Court's striking down of the sign law as yet another anti-minority violation of freedom would have been initially opposed, then grudgingly accepted in Quebec, as has happened with the past judicial rulings already cited in this book.

The likelihood that this would have happened was further enhanced by the Court's generous offering of a suggested compromise that it would have found acceptable: Instead of French-only signs, bilingual signs bearing both official languages would have been considered by the judiciary as a reasonable and "demonstrably justified" limitation under Charter section

....

90.   Peter H. Russell, Rainer Knopff and Ted Morton, Federalism and the Charter, Ottawa: Carleton University Press, 1993, pp. 557-559.

91.   Ibid.

1 on the section 2 right of freedom of speech. In fact, the Court openly acknowledged Quebec's legitimate right to preserve and promote the French language. The Court was even willing to accept a law requiring French lettering to be much larger than English, allowing French to visibly dominate without obliterating English on signs.   92.

          Quebec Premier Robert Bourassa was thus handed on a silver platter a compromise solution his separatists (who were difficult to please in any event) while keeping the Meech Lake Accord on track.. The remaining first ministers would have received a firm demonstration from Quebec that it was prepared to meet judicially-acceptable standards for protecting rights and freedoms. The sincere efforts and trust shared between the 11 first ministers could then have continued unabated.

          Unfortunately there was a troublesome fly in this political ointment: section 33. In the absence of the override clause, Bourassa would have had the political luxury of throwing his hands up in the air and announcing that the court had made its decision and there was nothing more he could do than to adopt a compromise measure the Court would accept.

          At least some of the blame from separatists would then have been directed at the courts while the larger public gave thought to the judicial reasons why

92.   Peter H. Russell, Rainer Knopff and Ted Morton, Federalism and the Charter, Ottawa: Carleton University Press, 1993, pp. 557-559.

the Bill 101 sign law was an unacceptable violation of national and provincial charters of rights.

The luxury inherent in all of this is that it comes close to becoming that most-cherished political option - a judicial reference case in which a government gladly hands to the courts a difficult issue that has proven difficult to resolve at the political level.

Yet, the mere existence of section 33 was enough to strip Bourassa of anything even resembling a reference case luxury. The Opposition in Quebec began clamouring to have section 33 invoked and pro-sign law demonstrations quickly gathered momentum with the mass realization that a judicial ruling from the highest court in the land was no longer the final word, that the unacceptable could be forcibly made acceptable, that an unconstitutional violation of rights could be made constitutional merely by invoking section 33, without doing anything to correct the original violation of rights.

Under pressure, with nothing approximating a 'reference case' escape route, Bourassa invoked section 33. Had Bourassa adopted the Court's suggested compromise, he would not only have avoided invoking the override and maintained the trust of the other first ministers, he would have kept an election promise to lift restrictions on the use of bilingual signs. That promise had helped his party get elected, attracted talented English-speaking politicians to the Liberal government and drew support from English-speaking Quebecers, while maintaining significant support from francophones.

Instead, Bourassa broke his promise and came up a unique compromise of his own: Under his Bill 178, Quebec would ban English from exterior commercial signs while allowing French-dominant bilingual signs inside stores.

Alas, Bourassa's compromise still violated freedom of expression and was unacceptable to the Court, to Anglophones, to Francophones (for not going far enough), to first ministers, to Canadians in general, to almost everyone, including some members of his own party: Three Anglophone cabinet ministers resigned.   93.

Bourassa invoked section 33 to prevent any court challenge of Bill 178 and in so doing, illustrated another glaring, practical flaw in the override clause: A perceived value of the notwithstanding clause is that it allows legislatures to override the Charter and 'correct' the Court from striking down legislation which conflicts with the Charter yet represents strong popular will.

Yet, there was very little popular support for Bill 178 - it was almost universally despised. The use

••

93.   Quebec v. Ford et al., In the Supreme Court of Canada. Judgement rendered Dec. 15, 1988., in Peter H. Russell, Rainer Knopff and Ted Morton, Federalism and the Charter, Ottawa: Carleton University Press, 1993, pp. 557-581.

of section 33 in this case not only perpetuated an otherwise unconstitutional violation of rights , it propped up a piece of legislation which could not legitimately claim popular support.

The political backlash from Bourassa's move was explosive. As Morton notes, "Bourassa's use of the section 33 override to reinstate restrictions on English-language advertising was widely criticized and contributed to the eventual defeat of the Meech Lake Accord."   94.

With Newfoundland and Manitoba complaining bitterly about Ottawa's heavy-handed bargaining approach and deep distrust towards Quebec, the Meech Lake Accord became unravelled, in the end, by Manitoba MPP Elijah Harper, an Aboriginal Canadian unhappy with the lack of native rights in the Accord, who used a procedural delaying tactic to scuttle a vote on the accord.   95.

This self-serving end to a constitutional accord was poetic justice given the self-serving, horse-trading approach the first ministers had exhibited, indulging in what Monahan earlier described as "raw political bargaining," to arrive at what Cairns aptly deemed the "blunt and brutal" compromise of section 33.

....

94.   F. L. Morton, Law, Politics and the Judicial Process, Calgary: University of Calgary Press, 1992, p 419.
95.   David Milne, The Canadian Constitution, Toronto: James Lorimer & Company Publishers, 1991, pp. 148-260.

Although a supporter of the override, partly on grounds it promotes legislature supremacy, Ajzenstat has also denounced the unseemly, disrespectful attitudes at work in the drafting of the Meech Lake and Charlottetown Accords, noting that drafters "expected to carve up 'constitutional stone' with as much ease as politicians carving up the proceeds of a patronage deal." 96.

Ajzenstat further observes that "the old idea that the constitution is above politics, and that constitutionally entrenched rights are well protected from the political process and the whims of particular interests is breaking down."
She warns that if the distinction between constitutional and ordinary law fails, "even the negative rights like free speech, freedom of assembly, and equality, will be subordinated to the push and shove of the political process and the will of the majority." 97.

As an opponent of section 33, let me state that I agree with the validity of Ajzenstat's warning and assert that Quebec's callous use of the override is solid evidence that freedom of expression is being "subordinated to the push and shove of the political process and the will of the majority."

....

96. Janet Ajzenstat, 'A Social Charter Eh? Thanks, But No Thanks', Hamilton: McMaster University Political Science essay, 1994, p. 9.
97. Ibid., pp. 9-10.

The courts correctly deemed Bill 178 to be an unreasonable violation of freedom of expression against the merchants, some with pre-Confederation roots in Quebec, whose only 'crime' was that they were advertising their own private businesses in the Official Language of their choice.

For many small business people, their business is more than their livelihood. It is their life. It is their identity. They were being told by Quebec to mask over their identity, to obliterate any visible sign of the centuries-old, English-Canadian presence in Montreal, so as not to offend any anti-English bigot who might wander by their store, so as not to lay bare the myth of a French-only province.

Conrad Black observes that many Canadians "feel betrayed by Bill 178," and that if not for this bill and the override, "the Meech Lake Accord would have gone through like an express train."   98.
Black notes the Accord was "assured of difficult passage when Brian Mulroney reacted so tepidly to Bill 178 that English Canadians concluded he had made a Faustian bargain with the premier of Quebec and was not serious about defending the linguistic rights of the majority of Canadians."   99.

....

98.   Conrad Black, 'Enough is Enough', in Canadian Politics 91/92, edited by Gregory s. Mahler and Roman R. March, Guilford, Connecticut: Dushkin Publishing Group, 1991, p. 6.
99.   Ibid.

Asserting that "rights dependent on the whim of ephemeral majorities among provincial legislators are illusory," Black concludes that:

> "The 'Notwithstanding clause should be revoked. No country can function when its highest courts, adjudicating the most vital questions of civil rights, are subject to revision and revocation by provincial legislatures. While that preposterous clause remains, there is nothing to stop any province from invoking, as Quebec did with Bill 178, the tawdry old Duplessis flimflam (resurrected by most of his successors, including Levesque and Bourassa) that collective rights take precedence over individual rights. This is a matrix for the complete conditionality and revocability of all rights, in matters of language as it was in matters of religious and political freedom when applied in Quebec to Jehovah's Witnesses, and to leftists under the Pad lock Law." 100.

The extent to which section 33 provides unwarranted provincial power over the Supreme Court while aiding an equally unhealthy drift into decentralization is examined in our next chapter.

....

100.   Conrad Black, 'Enough is Enough', in Canadian Politics 91/92, edited by Gregory s. Mahler and Roman R. March, Guilford, Connecticut: Dushkin Publishing Group, 1991, p. 6.

4

The Road to Decentralization

Canada was born of a centralist vision but has been on a decentralist trend since Confederation which threatens to irreparably harm our country. The substance of this threat - and section 33's contribution to it - will be explored in this chapter.

A unifying element countering the threat posed by province-builders and decentralist federalists has been Canada's unitary court system. As F. L. Morton explains:

> "A distinctive feature of the Canadian judicial system is its unitary character... While the Canadian Founders adopted the logic of federalism for the distribution of legislative authority they did not apply it to the judiciary. They created a single

judicial system to interpret and to apply both federal and provincial laws...both civil law, which is mainly provincial in origin, and criminal law, which is almost exclusively federal in origin, move from trial to appeal through the same system of courts. This unitary character of the Cana dian judicial system is politically signifi cant because it can mitigate the centrifugal forces of federal-provincial politics. Rather than accentuating regional differences, it promotes continuity and uniformity of legal policy across the nation." 101.

Morton, also notes that "the greater impact of the Charter on provincial law-making also supports earlier predictions about the potential of the Charter to act as a force for policy uniformity throughout Canada." He adds that Charter proponents hope it will serve a nation-building role. 102.

Yet, the unifying characteristics of both the judicial system and the Charter, which Morton re-ferred to, are now under attack from a new divisive entity - section 33.

Every time the override is used by a province it

....
101. F. L. Morton, Law, Politics and the Judicial Process, Calgary: 1992, p. 47.
102. Ibid., p. 419.

breaks the traditional unifying continuity of the courts by handing back to the province the final word on the violation of rights and freedoms.

The Charter's unifying featuresare similarly undermined.

Section 33 ensures that our commonly-shared, inalienable rights and freedoms are not necessarily commonly-shared or inalienable.

The English language is shared by Canadians across Canada, including those Canadians in Quebec where it is widely spoken as a second language.

Yet, Quebec has been able to use section 33 to violate freedom of expression and restrict the use of English in that part of Canada.

It is of little comfort that section 33 rights violations are so far small in number. The permanence of the override and Quebec's willingness to use it are cause for concern.

To the extent that section 33 can be used by provinces to overrule the federally-appointed Supreme Court and undermine what would otherwise be national standards and national rights and freedoms, the notwithstanding clause is fuelling the fires of decentralization and the incremental separation of Quebec.

It is a worrisome addition to the forces of disunity which plague our nation.

Of the Meech Lake Accord's decentralist features - giving Quebec distinct society status and control over immigration and the provinces new powers including the ability to approve or deny the creation of added provinces - Black finds Mulroney's rush into further decentralization "risked turning the orderly dismemberment of the federal state into a disembowelment." 103.

Observing that the degree of decentralization has now been carried to "absurd extremes," Black adds that "the fact that we seemed briefly to commit the future of Canada to a referendum in Newfoundland (with 2 per cent of our population) over whether Quebec is a distinct society - before delivering ourselves over to the histrionics of Chief Harper - emphasizes how fragile and anomalous our federal institutions have become." 104.

Romanow, Whyte and Leeson note a profound change is occurring in the way Canadians view their country, a view which relates directly to the original intent of our first prime minister:

"Canada is catching up to Macdonald. Less and less do Canadians see the country's

103. Conrad Black, 'Enough is Enough', in Canadian Politics 91/92, edited by Gregory S. Mahler and Roman R. March, Guilford, Connecticut: Dushkin Publishing Group, 1991, p. 6.
104. Ibid.

virtue to be its capacity to accommodate and nurture its many local political communities. More and more, Canada is seen to be a single political unit which, in its own right, has the responsibility and, now, the will to represent the interests of all." 105.

Indeed, Canada is a nation that began with a centralized vision but succumbed to an ongoing drift towards decentralization that has already made it the most decentralized country in the world.

The dangers of such an extensive degree of decentralization are considerable as the growth of provincial power at the expense of the federal government threatens to leave Canada a hollow shell with little presence on the world stage.

Garth Stevenson asserts that the extent to which Canada has decentralized is unhealthy.

Stevenson points out that "the picture that Canada presents to the outside world is that of an increasingly loose collection of semi-sovereign provinces, with a central government unable or unwilling to exercise much control over the economy or to carry out coherent policies even within its own fields of jurisdiction. Compared with almost any other

....

105. Roy Romanow, John Whyte, Howard Leeson, Canada Notwithstanding., Agincourt: Carswell/Methuen, 1984. p. xvii.

modern state, or with Canada itself as recently as the 1950s, the extent of provincial power and the passivity of the central government are remarkable." 106.

Stevenson concludes that Canada is today in a weakened position due to decentralization and a reversal of this trend may be needed to for the nation to fully function on the world stage:

> "Canada is a relatively small, industrialized country in a world where most of its com petitors are larger, stronger, and more central ized. If it is to survive in this environment and to overcome the divisive effects of its geographical barriers and its closeness to the United States, it may require a stronger central government that it has enjoyed in recent years and a corresponding reduction in the powers of provincial governments." 107.

Donald Smiley warns that the drift towards decentralization has left the federal government weak and without a central focus:

> "The price of such change ... has been a pro found absence of national direction. Without such direction and without any coherent na-

....

106. Garth Stevenson, 'Federalism and Intergovernmental Relations,' from Canadian Politics in the 1990s, Third Edition, edited by Michael S. Whittington and Glen Williams, (Toronto: Nelson Canada, 1990), pp. 397-398.
107. Ibid. p. 399.

tional vision articulated by the leadership of the federal parties, Canadian politics be comes little more than a 'scuffle of private interests'." 108.

Richard Simeon states that the federal government is finding it lacks sufficient powers to be fully effective on the international stage.

Simeon notes that federal power is "draining on the one hand to supra-national institutions and one the other to smaller local institutions (provinces) - the main federal levers have become more and more constrained." 109.

It appears likely that the provincial forays into international affairs and trade will increase in coming years. As Grant Reuber observes the provinces are working counter to the need for a strong federal government voice in international markets. He asserts that "all signs point to a substantial decentralization of power from Ottawa to the provinces." 110.

....

108. Donald V. Smiley, The Federal Condition In Canada, Toronto: McGrawHill Ryerson Ltd., 1987, p. 187.
109. Richard Simeon, 'Concluding Comments,' from Canadian Federalism: Meeting Global Economic Challenges?' edited by Douglas M. Brown and Murray G. Smith, Kingston: Queen's University, 1991, p. 287.
110. Grant L. Reuber, 'Federalism and Negative-Sum Games' from Confederation In Crisis, edited by Robert Young, Toronto: James Lorimer & Company, 1991, p. 50.

Section 33 adds to this destructive trend.

As Don Braid and Sydney Sharpe have observed, Prime Minister Pierre Trudeau faced a substantial threat of further decentralization through the
Section 33 Notwithstanding clause, a regional power-
enhancing device which "was the creation of three
former western premiers: Conservatives Peter
Lougheed of Alberta and Sterling Lyon of Manitoba,
and New Democrat Allan Blakeney of Saskatchewan."
Braid and Sharpe add:

>"Prime Minister Mulroney likes to blame
>Pierre Trudeau for this radical device, but
>in fact Trudeau was wary of the notwith
>standing clause, and accepted it only after
>the provinces agreed to a five-year sunset
>provision. Trudeau sensed, correctly, that
>Quebec would use the clause to promote its
>language policies and autonomy, and he
>surely knew the West would eventually
>employ it to whittle away central author
>ity."   111.

Braide and Sharpe note that Trudeau is not
alone in his distrust of Section 33:

>"Only in 1989, after Quebec overruled the
>Charter and many Canadians grew
>concerned, did Mulroney suddenly see

....
111.   Don Braide & Sidney Sharpe, Breakup: Why the West
feels Left Out of Canada, Toronto: Key Porter , 1990, p. 117.

dangers in the clause. He called for its abolition, but his chances for success are slim." 112.

As the preceding commentary indicates, Section 33 was a creation of provinces for the enhancement of provincial power.

Although potential use of the clause also extends to the federal government, this level of government has yet to make use of the clause and, as with the ancient right of disallowance, Section 33 lies in disuse in Ottawa.

Quebec has already made use (or abuse in this writer's view) of the non obstante clause. Braide and Sharpe suspect the western provinces may also utilize the clause.

There can be no question over the provincial power enhancement made possible by Section 33 as it gives provincial governments the ability to overrule not only their own courts, but also the Supreme Court of Canada, the highest court in the land.

For any province wishing to advance a province-building agenda at the expense of human rights, Section 33 is there to be used on a whim - as Quebec has already demonstrated.

....

112.   Don Braide & Sidney Sharpe, Breakup, Toronto: Key Porter, 1990, p 117.

Section 33 is another provincial building block in a country in which the provinces are already far too powerful in relation to the national government.

The notwithstanding clause can be seen as another step on a decentralist journey which has taken us tragically far away from the original centralist intent behind the formation of Canada.

To gain a fuller appreciation of the decentralist distance we have journeyed, a look back at Canadian history is helpful: A legislative deadlock between members of Canada East and Canada West, combined with distrust of the Americans (some of whom were calling for annexation of Canada at the end of the U.S. Civil War in 1865), and economic consider-ations flowing from the end of Reciprocity with the United States and British free trade policies, all bol-stered the idea of creating a larger union of British North American colonies.

The idea met with varying degrees of enthusi-asm, but on July 1, 1867 the provinces of Ontario, Quebec, Nova Scotia and New Brunswick freely joined together as the federal dominion of Canada and the new country grew from there with the addi-tion of more provinces to the collective whole.   113.

....

113.   George F. G. Stanley, A Short History of The Canadian Constitution, Toronto: Ryerson Press, 1969. pp. 74-80.

Under the Compact Theory of Confederation, the future provinces were autonomous colonies which delegated some of their power to the central government and the constitution should not be amended to alter the agreement which led the former colonies to enter Confederation.   114.

Yet, as the Task Force on Canadian Unity observed, the idea of two founding nations is fraught with divisive problems:

> "The native peoples (the country's real founders) understandably find the two-founding-peoples concept of duality offensive. English-speaking Canadians find it difficult to conceive of two nations and doubt there was a pact in 1867."   115.

Although Compact Theory and the concept of founding British and French races have been used by Quebec decentralists to argue for increased provincial power or even 'sovereignty', such concepts when looked at closely, fall short of encapsulating a full definition of Canada.

....

114.   Roy Romanow, John Whyte and Howard Leeson, Canada Notwithstanding. The Making of the Constitution 1976-1982, Agincourt: Carswell/Methuen Publishers, 1984. p. 168.
115.   The Task Force on Canadian Unity, A Future Together: Observations and Recommendations, Ottawa: Minister of Supply and Services, 1979, 21-22.

Our nation's whole clearly exceeds the sum of its parts as it not only combines provincial economies, but exercises powers the former colonies, with their limited autonomy, had never held, such as military and monetary functions that had been under purely British jurisdiction. Neither concept accounts for the addition of new provinces from former territories of non-British and non-French ethnicity.

While the role played in our early history by Canadians of British and French ancestry is historically significant, the notion that this should, in the 20th century, confer some sort of special status on those of British or French ancestry is offensive to anyone who believes all Canadians should be considered equals.

Quebec's divisive anti-English sign law - forcibly made constitutional by section 33 - undermines the unifying principle that Canadians, regardless of language, have existed as a people for more than a century and have evolved into a united, though culturally diverse, nation.

Indeed, Canada was always meant to be much more than some loose, early version of today's European Community, and the original intent of our Founding Fathers clearly illustrates the degree to which this is true.

There is no question that Sir John A. Macdonald, our first prime minister, had clearly envisioned a centralized and expansive Canada which, in fact, did expand to include other provinces.

Macdonald also drew a sharp distinction between the American sovereign states in their loose union and the centralized nature of Canada when he observed:

> "Here we have adopted a different system. We have strengthened the General Government. We have given the General Legislature all the great subjects of legislation. We have conferred on them, not only specifically and in detail, all the powers which are incident to sovereignty, but we have expressly declared that all subjects of general interest not distinctly and exclusively inferred upon the local governments and local legislatures, shall be conferred upon the General Government and Legislature. - We have thus avoided that great source of weakness which has been the cause of the disruption of the United States." 116.

George Brown observed that "we have thrown over on the localities all the questions which experience has shown lead directly to local jealously and discord, and we have retained in the hands of the

....

116.   Excerpt from the speech of John A Macdonald in Parliamentary Debates on the Subject of the Confederation of the British North American Provinces, 1865.

General Government, all the powers necessary to secure a strong and efficient administration of public affairs." 117.

W. P. M. Kennedy notes that "when John A Macdonald discovered that his outspoken preference for a unitary kingdom could not be realized, and that federalism alone would satisfy the diverse interests concerned, he bent his energies, with apparent support from his colleagues, to give to the new federation as strong a bias towards a unitary system as circumstances would allow." 118.

Although many of the 33 Fathers of Confederation were not entirely comfortable with the centralizing character of the Canadian union, there was no attempt to hide the degree of power given the federal government and it was an openly-centralist union which won sufficient support to come into being. 119

Noting that "no intention of the Fathers of Confederation was more clear than that the new nation was to have a strong central government," F. R.

....

117. Excerpt from the speech of George Brown in Parliamentary Debates on the Subject of Confederation of the British North American Provinces, 1865.

118. W. P. M. Kennedy, Essays in Constitutional Law, London: Oxford University Press, 1934, p 83.

119. J. M. Beck, The Shaping of Canadian Federalism: Central Authority or Provincial Right? Toronto: The Copp Clark Publishing Company, 1971. p. 7.

Scott observed that "in contrast to the American colonies, which approached union from the position of sovereign and independent states, and gave up their full powers with reluctance, the Canadian provinces came to union as colonies..."   120.

Scott added: "Several opponents of Confederation based their opposition precisely on the ground that there was too much centralization."   121.

Indeed, the degree of real and intended centralization was well known. The provinces clearly entered Confederation as junior partners. Describing the Constitution Act, 1867, as a "quasi-federal constitution," K. C. Wheare notes the supreme central federal government was given the power to disallow legislation passed by lower provincial governments.   122.

J. M. Beck observed disallowance - the ability of the federal government to overrule provincial legislation - was evidence of a centralized political structure that did not fit any strict definition of federalism and was clearly intended to keep the provinces subordinate to the national government.   123.

....

120.   F. R. Scott, 'Political Nationalism and Confederation,' Canadian Journal of Economics and Political Science, VIII , August, 1942, pp 399-400.
121.   Ibid. p. 402.
122.   K. C. Wheare, Federal Government, London: Oxford University Press, 1946, pp. 19-20.
123.   J. M. Beck, The Shaping of Canadian Federalism, Toronto: Copp Clark, 1971. pp 1-3.

The power of disallowance was also potentially important in the field of rights, for as George Brown has stated, disallowance provides a means by which an impartial central government can intervene to undo unjust provincial legislation.

However, most of the 112 times the federal government has applied disallowance since 1867 have been instances of the federal government merely defending its perceived jurisdiction from an ultra vires intrusion by provinces, rather than a bold protection of rights. Federal governments have long shown a reluctance to intervene in provincial actions and have demonstrated a preference to avoid using the disallowance clause in favor of either negotiation with provinces or referral to courts.   124.

From all of this we can see that the intent from the beginning was to fashion, from former British colonies, a nation with a strong central government. Writing in Canada's Centennial year, Donald Smiley succinctly noted that "a group of the political leaders of British North America agreed a century ago upon a constitutional, political and economic settlement which would establish a new nation on the northern half of the continent."   125.

....

124.   J. M. Beck, The Shaping of Canadian Federalism, Toronto: Copp Clark, 1971. pp 146-153.
125.   Donald Smiley, The Canadian Political Nationality, Toronto: Methuen Publications, 1967. p. 1.

Smiley's use of the word 'nation' is deliberate for what was being created in 1867 was a new political nation and political nationality, regardless of language and regional differences, from former colonies which became provinces under the British North America Act of 1867.   126.

Quebec also recognized that "in 1867 the distribution of powers contemplated in the British North America Act gave clear predominance to the federal government, which was assigned the main powers of the day in addition to certain residual powers and the right to repudiate any provincial law."   127.

Quebec also took an early lead in pushing for decentralization of powers from the federal government to the province. Garth Stevenson emphasizes the pivotal role Quebec has played in the advancement of provincial powers, noting: "The demands for provincial legislative powers came mainly from the French Canadians, for whom the establishment of a Quebec legislature was the major attraction of Confederation. The powers which they demanded for that legislature were mainly related to social institutions, education, the family, and the legal system."   128.

126.   Donald Smiley, The Canadian Political Nationality, Toronto: Methuen Publications, 1967. 2-7.

127.   Jean Allaire, et. al., A Quebec Free To Choose: Report of the Constitution Committee of the Quebec Liberal Party, January 28, 1991. p. 7.

128.   Garth Stevenson, Unfulfilled Union: Canadian Federalism and National Unity, Toronto: Gage Educational Publishing Company, 1989, p. 29.

Ontario also played an early role in decentralization. Oliver Mowat, premier from 1872-1896, has been called the Father of Provincial Rights for his successful efforts to expand Ontario's provincial boundaries and have lieutenant governors appointed by the provinces.   129.

In many ways, the provinces' push for decentralization arrived with the dawn of Confederation and simply gained momentum following 1867.   130.

Indeed, the mere existence of provinces has been enough to ensure some degree of decentralist province-building efforts will take place.

Quebec in particular has long endeavoured to assume greater provincial powers and enhanced control over its economy.   131.

Aiding this seemingly natural yen by provinces for more power was the Judicial Committee of the Privy Council, which was given a statutory

....

129.   Garth Stevenson, Unfulfilled Union: Canadian Federalism and National Unity, Toronto: Gage Educational Publishing Company, 1989, p. 29.

130.   J. Peter Meekison, 'The Amending Formula,' from Perspectives on Canadian Federalism, edited by R. D. Olling & M. W. Westmacott, Scarborough: Prentice Hall, 1988, p. 68.

131.   R. I. Cheffins & P.A. Johnson, The Revised Canadian Constitution, Toronto: McGraw-Hill Ryerson, 1986, p. 119.

basis by the Imperial Parliament in Britain to rule on jurisdictional disputes between the federal government and the provinces.

In a vast majority of cases, the JCPC proved sympathetic to provincial arguments for more power and usually ruled in favor of the provinces. As Garth Stevenson notes, Sir John A. Macdonald was to find that "the Judicial Committee's decisions were to play a decisive part in undermining his plans for a highly centralized federation." 132.

Despite the original intent of a strong central government, the provinces convinced the JCPC that provinces were not meant to be subordinate to the federal government, but equal.

As Robert Vipond notes: "the provincialists argued that real federalism requires a balanced division of power in which neither level overwhelms the other. In this sense, federalism implies political parity, and the autonomists argued that the division of powers outlined in sections 91 and 92 of the BNA Act established a rough balance between national and provincial powers respectively." 133.

.

132.   Garth Stevenson, Unfulfilled Union. Canadian Federalism and National Unity, Toronto: Gage Educational Publishing Company, 1989, pp. 46-47.
133.   Robert C. Vipond, Liberty and Community: Canadian Federalism and the Failure of the Constitution, Albany: State U. of New York Press, 1991, p 5.

Peter Russell, Rainer Knopff and Ted Morton observe that "in a series of cases the Privy Council evolved a number of implied limitations which had the effect of reducing the federal commerce power in Canada to a pale shadow of its counterpart in the United States' Constitution." 134.

The decentralization trend would continue long past the JCPC's 1949 departure from Canadian judicial politics. Except for a brief period in our history, in the 1950s through early 1970s, the story of Canada is one of constant devolution of powers from the federal government to the provinces. Section 33 has further fueled this unhealthy province-building trend.

The election of the Parti Quebecois in November 1976 brought a renewed sense of urgency to constitutional reform and an expanded threat of decentralization. As Romanow, Leeson and Whyte explain:

"While highlighting the need for constitutional reform, the election in Quebec provoked conflicting reactions. On the one hand, it was recognized that the struggle for autonomy to be waged by the Parti Quebecois could aid the decentralization ambitions harbored by the provinces. On the other hand, there was great

....

134.   Peter H. Russell, Rainer Knopff and Ted Morton, Federalism and the Charter, Ottawa: Carleton University Press, 1993, p 32.

98

uncertainty how far such decentralization should be urged before it assumed unde sirable or unmanageable proportions. Moreover, western alienation was exacer bated by Ottawa's increasing tendency to focus reform on the needs of Quebec." 135

Trudeau recognized the potentially destructive forces of decentralization, separation and alienation when he observed: "It is this loyalty to the whole country upon which we must build if we want to vanquish the enemy within, this gnawing doubt, this uncertainty as to whether or not we will continue in ten or 20 years to act as a strong united nation..." 136

Decentralization of powers, in Trudeau's view, had only led to demands from the provinces - particu- larly Quebec - for still more powers at the expense of the federal government and its weakened ability to unite the nation. Decentralization had weakened the central ties that bind, and, by making the provinces more powerful, had resulted in a looser federation with an enhanced threat of Quebec separation. 137

....

135.   Roy Romanow, John Whyte & Howard Leeson, Canada Notwithstanding. Agincourt: 1984. p. xix.

136.   Excerpt from a speech by Pierre Trudeau, House of Commons Debates, 32nd Parliament, First session, April 15, 1980.

137.   Richard Gwyn, The Northern Magus: Pierre Trudeau and Canadians, Toronto: McClelland and Stewart, 1980, p 53.

However, Trudeau's centralist approach was overturned by the Brian Mulroney Progressive Conservative government of the 1980s through early 1990s which replaced FIRA with Investment Canada which greatly reduced federal control over foreign investment.

Mulroney also tried unsuccessfully to enact two different constitutional accords - Meech Lake and Charlottetown - which would have succeeded in further decentralizing federal power to the provinces while recognizing Quebec as a distinct society.

Indeed, the Mulroney drift towards decentralization has been remarkable. As Janine Brody observes:
"The drama of politics in the past decade is, in many ways, a chronicle of how the Conservative party succeeded in forging new regional alliances in order to displace the Liberals and thereby realize their version of a decentralized, continentalist and market-driven economy." 138.

Quebec has taken to exerting previously unseen provincial power: The province's decision to invoke the notwithstanding clause in the Charter of Rights in

....

138.   Janine Brodie, 'Tensions from Within: Regionalism and Party Politics in Canada', from Party Politics in Canada 6th Edition, edited by Hugh G. Thorburn, Scarborough: Prentice-Hall Canada, 1991, p. 231.

order to overturn the ruling of the Supreme Court of Canada that Quebec's Law 101 prohibiting the use of English on exterior store signs was an unconstitutional violation of the basic human right of freedom of expression.   139.

Insofar as Section 33 effectively confers on the provinces new power which can be used to overrule the highest courts in the nation, it is an unwelcome addition to an unhealthy decentralization trend.

For reasons discussed earlier in this chapter, the degree of decentralization in Canada has already made our nation the most decentralized country in the world and any further movement in this direction would only further weaken an already weak federal government.

Canada needs to have a credible presence on the world stage.

The Supreme Court of Canada must have its judicial rulings on matters of rights and freedoms accorded the respect they deserve.

It is unacceptable that separatist or quasi-separatist premiers should so easily avail themselves

....

139.   Reg Whitaker, 'The Overriding Right,' from Canadian Politics 91/92, edited by Gregory S. Mahler and Roman R. March, Guilford, Conn.: Dushkin Publishing, 1991, p. 37.

to a notwithstanding clause which allows them to push the courts aside in their zeal to violate rights and pursue an agenda that runs counter to individual and national interests.

Section 33 is not only contributing to decentralization, it is also assisting the incremental separation of Quebec from Canada - and this very real threat will be explored in detail in the next chapter.

5

THE QUEBEC PROBLEM

Compelling questions surround Quebec's decision to overrule the highest court in Canada by invoking section 33 expressly to violate the freedom of expression rights of English Speaking Canadians in that province.

Why did Quebec take this course of action?

What harm did Quebec see in allowing Canadians the right to advertise their own private business in the Official Language of their choice?

Why were Bill 178 and use of the override seen as necessary by Quebec?

Quebec Premier Robert Bourassa ignored a workable, generous compromise offered by the Court to instead take a heavy-handed, punitive approach to a minority's individual rights.

By many accounts, already cited in this book, Bourassa's actions poisoned the trust and good will the rest of Canada had shown towards Quebec and contributed to scuttling Meech Lake Accord - and possibly Charlottetown Accord - efforts to welcome Quebec into a constitution it was already legally a part of.

Following the failure of Meech Lake, Quebec released two important political reports falsely claiming Quebec's rejection by Canada and asserting the "need" for major decentralization to preserve Quebec culture.

Yet, both reports also recognized the important contribution made by English-speaking Canadians in Quebec.

The governing Quebec Liberal Party's Allaire report carried praise for the province's English-speaking community, noting that "its important contribution to the development of Quebec society is reflected in all spheres of activity, e.g. economy and finance, primary and secondary schools, colleges and universities, hospitals, the media, museums, architecture and so on." 140.

....
140. Jean Allaire, et. al., A Quebec Free To Choose: Report of the Constitution Committee of the Quebec Liberal Party, January 28, 1991. p. 18.

The Allaire report also spoke of the need to "safeguard the recognized historic rights of anglophone Quebeckers and specifically the right to their own social and cultural institutions along with the right to manage their development."   141.

Quebec's all-party Belanger-Campeau report similarly noted that "the English-speaking community has been historically part of Quebec's reality," and added that "its significant contribution to Quebec's development must be stressed and continue to be recognized."   142.

Given all of this post-Bill 178 recognition of English-speaking Canadians, why did Quebec earlier invoke the notwithstanding clause in an attempt to obliterate any visible commercial sign of these cherished citizens? As Mordecai Richler points out, Bill 178 also restricted francophone businesses in their use of English - a rights violation that infuriated those in tourism industries.   143.

Calling Bourassa's use of section 33 as "his betrayal of the anglophones in his province," P. K. Kuruvilla

....

141.   Jean Allaire, et. al., A Quebec Free To Choose: Report of the Constitution Committee of the Quebec Liberal Party, January 28, 1991. p. 32.

142.   Michel Belanger, Jean Campeau, et. al., Report of The Commission On The Political and Constitutional Future of Quebec, March 1991, Bureau d'information a Montreal, Sherbrooke, p. 66.

143.   Mordecai Richler, Oh Canada! Oh Quebec!, Requiem For a Divided Country, Toronto: Penguin Books, 1992, pp. 115-116.

notes the Court "while conceding the importance of safeguarding predominant status of the French language and culture in Quebec, had cautioned him in no uncertain terms that he could promote the preponderance of French, but not at the expense of the freedom of expression of the anglophones and other non-francophones in his province."   144.

If section 33 was invoked to 'protect' Quebec culture, what is its culture? Entering Confederation in 1867 Quebec rested on distinctive cultural pillars: It was agrarian, semi-feudal, inward-looking, almost unilingually French-speaking, Roman Catholic and with French Civil Code of law.   145.

Yet, all cultures change. Quebec's culture, like Ontario's, shifted from being agrarian - with all of the lifestyle, values and viewpoints this entails - to become a modern industrial society, with all of the values, lifestyles and viewpoints that this also entails.

Trudeau notes that French Civil law, initially a major difference between Quebec and the rest of Canada, today "occupies a very small place in the total picture of provincial laws by which we in Quebec are governed." Trudeau adds that Quebec's provincial laws are "the product of a judicial

....

144. Dr. P. K. Kuruvilla, 'Quebec's Action Was Wrong', from Policy Options, Vol. 10, No. 4, May 1989, Halifax: The Institute for Research on Public Policy, p. 7.
145. Bayard Reesor, The Canadian Constitution in Historical Perspective, Prentice Hall Canada Inc., Scarborough: 1992. pp. 3-12.

culture far more closely related to that of the other provinces than to the laws of New France or the Napoleonic Code." 146.

Quebec shifted away from being semi-feudal and inward-looking although for years the province clung to an "illiberalism," which Charles Taylor suggests was "seemingly organized around the values of a traditional, ultramontane Catholicism." 147. Taylor says illiberalism grew into the late 1950s:

> "The ravages of Maurice Duplessis on the rule of law, which he seemed to get away with - his treatment of Jehovah's witnesses and Communists - seemed to indicate that Quebec and French Canada had different views about the toleration of dissent. Some people were ready to be lieve that the two societies gave quite different values to the maintenance of unity around certain cherished truths and standards when these conflicted with the goods of tolerance, freedom or permitted diversity." 148.

....

146. Pierre Trudeau, 'The Poverty of Nationalist Thinking in Quebec', in Towards A Just Society, edited by Thomas S. Axworthy and Pierre Elliott Trudeau, Toronto: Penguin Books, 1992, p. 434.
147. Charles Taylor, 'Shared and Divergent Values', in Options for a New Canada, edited by Ronald L. Watts and Douglas M. Brown, Toronto: University of Toronto Press, 1991, p. 53.
148. Ibid.

Yet as Taylor also notes, "this difference has disappeared today." He suggests that "partly one might say that French Canada has rejoined 'English Canada': more accurately, one might say that the forces within Quebec that were always striving for a liberal society have won out."   149.

Taylor finds "a remarkable similarity throughout the country, and across the French-English difference, when it comes to the things in life which are important." He adds "when it comes to the values that specifically relate to political culture, there seems to be broad agreement: about equality, non-discrimination, the rule of law, the mores of representative democracy, about social provision, about violence and firearms, and a host of issues."   150.

Taylor also notes that "some English-speaking Canadians seem still to doubt this, to harbour a suspicion of Quebec's liberal credentials, but this is quite unfounded in the 1990s - or rather, suspicions are in order, but just as they are about any other Atlantic society, for none of these is exempt from racism, chauvinism, and similar ills."   151.

....

149.   Charles Taylor, 'Shared and Divergent Values', in Options for a New Canada, edited by Ronald L. Watts and Douglas   M. Brown, Toronto: University of Toronto Press, 1991, p. 53.
150.   Charles Taylor, 'Shared and Divergent Values', in Options for a New Canada, edited by Ronald L. Watts and Douglas M. Brown, Toronto: University of Toronto Press, 1991, p. 53.
151.   Ibid., p. 54..

In the main, Taylor is right that post-Duplessis Quebec has flowered into an egalitarian, liberal, outward-looking, modern secular province like the others. This is why this writer and other political observers have found Quebec's Bill 178 and use of the override so despicable in the fullest sense of the word: It is an aberration, a throwback to the Duplessis dark age when trampling rights was in fashion, a betrayal of the liberal values Quebec adopted. On the whole, Quebec remains a liberal society - but with a periodic tendency to violate rights which requires vigilance.

Once almost unilingually French-speaking, Quebec is today remarkably bilingual. As a former frequent visitor to Quebec, I can attest to the fact that one can get by with English not only in Montreal but in some of the most remote areas of Quebec, near the Atlantic Ocean and as far north as Labrador. French dominates in Quebec but the degree of English as a second language affirms that Canadians are bound by a common language from coast to coast to coast (Quebec also has one of Canada's largest anglophone populations outside of Ontario, BC and Alberta).

Thus we can see that Quebec's culture has indeed changed. Almost every pillar which initially defined this culture has disappeared. Quebec has gone from agrarian to industrial, from Roman Catholicism to secularism, semi-feudalism to liberalism, unilingualism to bilingualism, even its jurisprudence has changed to better reflect the Canadian whole and I should add that Quebec francophones now play a larger role in the province's business community than ever before. It makes little sense then for societal elites to attempt to freeze aspects of a culture which is wont to evolve. Yet this is what Quebec politicians have strived to do.

We need not dwell on the failed attempts of the Montreal school board to expel students caught speaking English on the playground.

It is of more interest to note that Law 101 requires francophone parents to send their children to French language schools. What should be a matter of choice has become a matter of law, apparently based on the unrealistic fear that if given the chance, francophones would cease to perpetuate the French language in Quebec. It is a pointless curtailment of freedom to shore up the French language when it is in no danger of disappearing from Quebec.

Yet it is also indicative of the fearful, overreactions - such as Bill 178 and the override- we've come to expect from Quebec governments which view the natural evolution of Quebec-Canadian culture as some sort of threat.

At the root of 'nationalist' thinking in Quebec is the notion that the discredited two founding races concept of Confederation holds some modern day importance - even though it has never been relevant for the western half of our country.

More disturbing is the idea that after 127 years of living together as a single people in Canada, the two founding races still exist and the Quebecois race is therefore deserving of special powers. It is an idea that demotes our country to little more than an economic arrangement while marginalizing the value of Canadians of non-French or non-British ancestry.

It also raises the question of who belongs to this distinct Quebecois society. Trudeau, noting that Quebec wanted the distinct society clause to be based on a French-speaking majority with a unique culture and civil law tradition, suggests "there is a very good chance then that Quebeckers of Irish, Jewish, Haitian or Vietnamese origin - even if they speak perfect French- would have trouble claiming to belong to this 'distinct' society." 152.

Richler hits the nail more bluntly on the head when he states Jews feel betrayed by Bill 178 and "Jews who have been Quebeckers for generations understand only too well that when thousands of flag-waving nationalists march through the streets roaring 'Le Quebec aux Quebecois!' they do not have in mind anyone named Ginsburg - or MacGregor, come to think of it." 153.

....

152.   Pierre Trudeau, 'The Poverty of Nationalist Thinking in Quebec', in Towards A Just Society, edited by Thomas S. Axworthy and Pierre Elliott Trudeau, Toronto: Penguin Books, 1992, p. 436.
153.   Mordecai Richler, Oh Canda! Oh Quebec!, Requiem For A Divided Country, Toronto: Penguin Books, 1992, p. 77.

Insisting Quebec is an open, pluralistic society, the Belanger-Campeau commission nonetheless objected to both the lack of constitutional recognition of duality and to references to the multicultural heritage of Canadians. It thus tried to perpetuate an outdated, false notion of two founding races, a notion which drives a wedge between Canadians.   154.

The commission also reported the terms 'province' and 'French Canadian' had fallen into disuse as citizens now regarded themselves as Quebeckers. 155.

As a journalist with over 20 years experience and some familiarity with Quebec, let me suggest here one's nationality doesn't fall into disuse - but it can be pushed into disuse through an array of measures, such as affixing the word 'national' to everything that is only provincial, such as arguing for 'sovereignty' when your citizens already enjoy sovereignty at provincial and federal levels of government, such as teaching school children a remarkably slanted version of Canadian history in which Quebec plays perpetual victim. I am also aware that objectivity is of little value to some of my colleagues in the Quebec media who hold membership in separatist parties and never report on the benefits of federalism. This is not to

....

154.   Michel Belanger, Jean Campeau, et. al., Report of The Commission On The Political and Constitutional Future of Quebec, March 1991, Bureau d'information a Montreal, Sherbrooke, p. 29.
155.   Ibid., pp. 12-19.

suggest a conspiracy is at work - it is not that organized. Rather, Canada has become a convenient scapegoat for whatever ails you in Quebec.

When it becomes difficult to put a finger on what Canada has done wrong, yet another airing of six people (half of them from Quebec) wiping their feet on a Quebec flag or a lone Aboriginal Manitoban MP scuttling Meech is sufficient for Quebec politicians to claim rejection by all of Canada. It is the basic dishonesty behind so many of Quebec's overblown claims of humiliation and rejection and its largely-unchallenged assertions that it needs more power to protect French that are worrisome.

Few federal politicians are willing to question Quebec demands as the price for doing so is to risk alienating a large bloc of votes and be accused of fuelling separatism. Thus, unending Quebec calls for power are politely accepted in Ottawa in what Trudeau aptly calls the blackmail of Canada.   156.

Perhaps the greatest poverty of nationalist thinking in Quebec today is that it perpetuates the image of the French Canadian as the conquered loser, rather than as the modern day offspring of Canadians

....

156.   Pierre Trudeau, 'The Poverty of Nationalist Thinking in Quebec', in Towards A Just Society, edited by Thomas S. Axworthy and Pierre Elliott Trudeau, Toronto: Penguin Books, 1992, p. 441.

who played, and continue to play, a crucial role in the development of Canada. This 'nationalism' has created something of an inferiority complex among Quebeckers and has prompted the anti-English-Canadian invocation of section 33. As Trudeau observes:

> "Under the Charter, all Canadians stand as equals before the state. But Quebec's nationalist elites, who are fearless in the face of competition from the United States and even the whole world, are scared stiff of English Canada. Only in the St. Jean Baptiste parade are we a race of giants; when the next day dawns and we come to measure ourselves against other Canadians as individuals, we are afraid we are not equal but inferior to them, and we run and hide behind our 'collective' rights which, if need be, we invoke to override the fundamental rights of 'others'. But what politicians or academic or businessperson will tell us which collectivity is supposed to have those rights?... are we dealing with a frankly racist notion that makes second or third class citizens of everyone but 'old stock' Quebeckers?"   157.

....

157.   Pierre Trudeau, 'The Poverty of Nationalist Thinking in Quebec', in Towards A Just Society, edited by Thomas S. Axworthy and Pierre Elliott Trudeau, Toronto: Penguin Books, 1992, pp. 436-7.

The myth that Quebec needs sweeping powers to survive intact has led to decentralizing proposals from the province, including the Allaire report.

Stating that "one of the objectives will be to reduce substantially the size of the central government," the Allaire report advocates exclusive Quebec authority over social affairs, municipal affairs, agriculture, unemployment insurance, communications, culture, regional development, education, energy, environment, housing, industry and commerce, language, recreation and sports, manpower, family policy, research and development, natural resources, health, public security, income security, and tourism plus a strong degree of shared authority over Native affairs, taxation and revenue, immigration (Quebec controls selection and integration, Canada handles health and security and refugees), financial institutions, and justice (Canada retains criminal law while Quebec controls civil law and the administration of justice and the courts).

The nationally-unifying unitary court system would be scrapped as "decisions of Quebec superior courts will no longer be subject to appeal to the Supreme Court of Canada," (thus the highest court in the land would no longer apply to Quebec), fisheries (inshore for Quebec - offshore to Canada), foreign policy, post office and telecommunications and transport.

"As far as the co-ordinating functions are concerned, the decisions of Parliament will have to be ratified by the Quebec National Assembly and the assemblies of the all the other legislatures (provincial or regional) that have adopted the same approach as Quebec." Exclusive federal authority is limited to defence, customs & tariffs, currency and common debt and equalization payments. Even in these areas, Quebec demands input, federal-provincial co-ordination and institutional restraints to limit federal action. "As for foreign policy, Quebec and Canada will finally benefit from a concerted approach."   158.

The Belanger-Campeau report similarly advocated a decentralist transformation of Canada which would leave the federal government a hollow shell unable to function on the world stage.

Its assumptions that federalism is a failed experiment in Canada were opposed by only a few of the report's contributors, including two politicians.

The comments are worth noting because they represent a pro-federal view of Canada which rarely gets heard in Quebec where even the so-called 'moderate' Liberal government of Bourassa has fanned the flames of separatism.

Jean-Pierre Hogue, a former MP for a Quebec riding: wished that the report put more emphasis on positive benefits Quebec has gained from Confedera

....

158.   Jean Allaire, et. al., A Quebec Free To Choose: Report of the Constitution Committee of the Quebec Liberal Party, January 28, 1991. p. 38-42.

tion, adding "I firmly believe that Quebecers do not want to break up the country they took centuries to build." 159.

Richard B. Holden said the report and its underlying premises "not only diminish the great achievements that Quebec has experienced while an integral part of Canada, but ...does not reflect the best interests of Quebec's citizens." In calling for a repeal of the section 33, Holden also cited the report's "false belief that the federal system and minorities threaten the flourishing and survival of the French language and culture in Quebec - all evidence demonstrates the contrary." 160.

Andre Ouellet: notes that "the commission fails to mention that Quebec's progress has been made within Canada." Ouellet reminds us that Quebec has been able to prosper in Canada since 1867 and thanks to federalism now enjoys one of the highest standards of living in the world. He also notes that the people of Quebec "voted massively" for the governments of King, Saint-Laurent and Pearson who adopted national policies helping the sick, unemployed and aged, yet now the federal government is being regarded as intrusive. 161.

....

159.   Michel Belanger, Jean Campeau, et. al., Report of The Commission On The Political and Constitutional Future of Canada and Quebec.
160.   Ibid., pp. 120-123.
1.   Ibid. pp. 124-125.

Unfortunately, the view that Canada has been a nurturing influence for the French fact - through bilingualism programs, grants, and an enormous amount of attention - doesn't receive much consideration in Quebec where it is assumed a province has an unalienable right to self-determination - even though it is merely a part of a large democratic nation which actually does hold that right.

The danger inherent in the pro-Canada message not getting through is that many young Quebeckers may rush into separation for all the wrong reasons.

How many have considered that this step would forever transform Quebec from being the most influential province in Canada - and the source of most of our prime ministers - into an irrelevant protectorate and minor trading partner?

Yet the separatist myths continue: Bloc Quebecois Leader Lucien Bouchard falsely told Washington officials that a solemn promise to Quebec had been broken three times, once by Trudeau who promised renewed federalism, twice more by the failed Meech Lake and Charlottetown accords.

As William Johnson points out, renewed federalism was not a promise for "a reform that would have satisfied Bouchard," while "Elijah Harper broke no promise to Quebecers when he vetoed Meech Lake in Manitoba. Johnson adds that Canadians broke no promise to Quebecers when, like Quebecers, they rejected the Charlottetown Accord as a bad deal."

Worse, Bouchard repeated the myth that a 50 per cent approval is sufficient for separation when major constitutional changes always require at least a two-thirds vote approval.   162.

The false messages of betrayal and humiliation fostered by separatists are unfortunately left unchallenged by federal politicians for fear of alienating Quebec.

Equally unfortunately, these myths take on the ring of truth over time and lend an artificial air of legitimacy to Quebec assertions that it must have more powers to protect the French fact and use the override if need be.

The Allaire report asserts that the Meech Lake Accord's failure was seen as "further proof that it was impossible for Quebec to obtain, within the existing federal structure, the powers essential to its survival and full development as North America's only francophone society."   163.

Survival? Allaire is referring to a francophone society that existed for centuries with far fewer powers than it has today. As Kuruvilla notes, "the

....

162.   William Johnson, '50% and we're gone:' Bouchard myths again', in The Hamilton Spectator, March 10, 1994, p. A9.
163.   Jean Allaire, et. al., A Quebec Free To Choose: Report of the Constitution Committee of the Quebec Liberal Party, January 28, 1991. p. 3.

alleged frailty of the French language and culture in North America cannot be by any stretch of the imagination a totally new phenomenon." Kuruvilla states Quebec was wrong to invoke section 33 to violate minority rights. He asks: "Having ostensibly survived all historical hostile forces and even prospered for over a century, does Quebec now have to go out of its way to extinguish minority language rights and help fan the flames of francophone nationalism?"   164.

Kuruvilla also asks "why did Quebec's Charter of Rights take the trouble of promising freedom of expression to all Quebecers in the first place? Why did the Liberal party in Quebec bother to include bilingualism as major plank in its platform until recently? Why did Bourassa make his election pledge in 1985 to make French dominant on signs but not to forbid other languages?"   165.

Kuruvilla also notes that other provinces have been "bestowing more educational and other rights on their francophone minorities," adding that it is "unfortunate that at a time when the rest of Canada has been assiduously attempting to make more accommodation and steadily stretching the hand of goodwill and neighbourliness, Quebec under both the Parti Quebecois and the Liberals has been stubbornly spurning it and sowing the seeds of discord between its francophone and anglophone communities."   166.

....

164.   Dr. P. K. Kuruvilla, 'Quebec's Action Was Wrong', from Policy Options, Vol. 10, No. 4, May 1989, Halifax: The Institute for Research on Public Policy, p. 7.
165.   Ibid.
166.   Ibid., p. 8.

Black notes that Bourassa, "a conditional federalist" has a view of Canada "that has never transcended basic arithmetic," as it is based on "profitable federalism" for Quebec within a Canadian common market - as opposed to the country of Canada.   167.

Observing that it is "difficult to comprehend the rationale and propriety of a supposedly non-separatist party callously raising the spectre of separatism as soon as its own cultural agenda begins to clash with that of the rest of the country."

Kuruvilla warns that "the Supreme Court has already categorically rejected the notion that the collective rights of francophones must have priority over individual rights in the Charter - one might also ask: suppose the anglophone majority in the country is inclined to adopt an insensitive and undemocratic attitude towards francophones in Quebec and elsewhere, what would be the ramifications for francophones?"   168.

Kuruvilla suggests that "it is very unlikely that the minority rights...would have existed merely because of the good nature and generosity of the government of Quebec." He adds:

> "On the contrary, these rights may have been grudgingly tolerated until now

....

167.   Conrad Black, 'Enough is Enough', Canadian Politics 91/92, edited by G. S. Mahler & R. March, Guilford: 1991, p.6.
168.   Dr. P. K. Kuruvilla, 'Quebec's Action Was Wrong', in Policy Options, Halifax: May 1989, p. 8.

simply because they were constitutionally stipulated at the inception of the federa tion. Fortunately for the minorities, the   BNA Act did not contain a notwithstand ing clause which a Quebec government could have blissfully exploited whenever it wished, as Mr. Bourassa is now able to do."   169.

Kuruvilla warns against the potential outcome of Quebec's unchecked province-building:

> "It is obvious that our political system is predicted on the lofty presumption that its constituent parts, while pursuing their legitimate self-interest, would show re spect for the needs of the country as a whole and make necessary compromises however difficult they might be, in order to strengthen the sinews of its nation hood. However, the government of Que bec at the present time seems to be almost exclusively concerned about its own future and not the future of Canada ...
> Needless to say, if it continues to be parochially preoccupied with province-building only and no nation-building at all, sooner or later, Canada as we know it today will have to ceasd to exist, with Quebec no more ... a part of it." 170

169.   Dr. P. K. Kuruvilla, 'Quebec's Action Was Wrong', in Policy Options, Halifax: May 1989, p. 8.
170.   Ibid.

Black asserts that Quebec is clearly taking the wrong route when it tries to shore up the French fact by oppressing the rights of other Canadians through Section 33. He notes that "the answer to Quebec's demographic problems must be seen to lie in raising the birth rate or providing incentives for French-language immigration, not in insane and insufferable affronts to other cultures and assaults on the rights of everyone."   171.

Black concludes "the real source of Quebec's population concerns is that, in rejecting their traditional society, Quebeckers threw the baby out with the bath water and the birth rate collapsed." He adds:

> "Quebec cannot have negative population growth, fail to attract assimible immi grants, and still expect to retain a constant proportion of the Canadian population. It cannot, as the saying goes, have it all. Commercial signs, of course, have nothing to do with it ..."   172.

Black also asserts that "the French will have to stop pretending that Quebec's English-speaking minority of more than 700,000 is other than the local extension of seventy-five per cent of Canadians and, linguistically, over ninety per cent of North Americans, which has exercised rights, not privileges, in Quebec for nearly a quarter of a millennium."   173.

....

171.   Conrad Black, 'Enough is Enough', Canadian Politics 91/92, eds. G. S. Mahler and R. March, Guilford: 1991, p.9.
172.   Ibid.
173.   Ibid.

There are those who cling to notions that section 33, unlike all the other powers Quebec has acquired and is demanding, is sufficient to satisfy the province.

Whitaker suggests that it would be folly to remove Section 33 now because "if the notwithstanding clause did not exist to protect 101 or its successors, independence would once again become a viable option." 174.

In fact, independence has become a viable option despite Section 33, as the Allaire report and the rise of the Bloc Quebecois have shown. Quebec has acquired formerly federal powers over pensions and immigration to cite but two examples.

Milne notes Quebec has instilled a significant the degree of asymmetry in Canada. Quebec can opt out of a number of constitutional ammendments while the use of the notwithstanding clause - so far only applied by provinces - is in practice asymmetric.
As well, Quebec alone collects corporate and individual taxes. Quebec has opted out of special welfare, youth allowance and even national student loans programs.   175.

....

174.   Reg Whitaker, 'The Overriding Right', from Policy Options, Halifax: May 1989, p. 4.
175.   David Milne, 'Equality or Asymmetry: Why Choose?', in Options for a New Canada, edited by Ronald L. Watts and Douglas M. Brown, Toronto: University of Toronto Press, 1991, pp. 290-291

The province is engaging in an incremental separatism which shows no sign of ending.

As Trudeau has so stated, giving Quebec more powers only leads to demands for more in a game of blackmail, via constant threats of separation.

Section 33 allows Quebec to behave more like a sovereign nation than a province because it allows it to overrule the highest court in the country and in so doing, only whets Quebec's appetite for more power.

As Peter Brimelow asserts, Quebec's Bill 178 and use of the override starkly "brought home to many English Canadians the obvious truth that Quebec is not playing the bi-national game, that its entire political elite is crypto-separatist."   176.

Brimelow concludes Quebec's Liberals and Parti Quebecois are headed for separation of Quebec, adding that "there is a high road and a low road, but they both lead to the same place."   177.

Sadly, Brimelow appears to be right about Quebec separation.

We should not the let the myths and self delusion practised by Quebec lull us into believing there is

....

176.   Peter Brimelow, 'The Maple Leaf For Ever?', in Canadian Politics 91/92, edited by Gregory S. Mahler and Roman R. March, Guilford Connecticut: Dushkin Publishing, 1991, p. 17.
177.   Ibid.

something noble in its ceaseless quest for more power at federal government expense.

Quebec is engaged in an intensely selfish exercise with little regard to its impact on Canada or on the freedoms of minorities which are there to be trampled if they conflict with the mythology of a French-only province.

This situation is especially intolerable for roughly a million English-speaking Canadians who reside in Quebec. Many of these Canadians have roots in Quebec that go back generations. And now they find their provincial government is using section 33 to overrule the highest courts in the land - all so human rights can be violated without recourse.

That this misuse of section 33 is via a 'moderate' government raises grave concerns for the future of rights in Quebec - and by extension, all of Canada.

Are we destined to become a polarized nation where English-speaking Canadians become second-class citizens the moment they set foot in Quebec?

6

CONCLUSIONS

As we've seen from the analysis of dozens of prominent political scientists cited in this paper, the Charter's section 33 override clause was the ill-conceived product of raw bargaining, a "blunt and brutal compromise," to again quote Cairns, with little thought given as to how it might be used in practice.

It was an incongruous, 11th hour addition to a constitutionally-entrenched Canadian Charter of Rights and Freedoms, an addition which undermined the Charter's ability to fully protect our rights from the whims of government.

Although initially attractive to some as a uniquely Canadian device for upholding the principle of legislative supremacy, section 33's callous and controversial use by Quebec provided a disturbing illustration of the harm that can be caused when a provincial government, pursuing a course running counter to Canada's national interests, receives unwarranted power to push forward dubious 'collectivist rights' goals while tossing aside individual freedoms meant to be protected by the Charter.

Noting that "the override has been defended as a uniquely Canadian way of reconciling judicial review with democratic accountability and decried as an unprincipled and tawdry political compromise that undermines the protection of rights," Vipond encapsulates a core area of concern.

Vipond further observes that "the controversy over the status and use of the override has reinforced the legitimacy of viewing the constitution as if it posed a stark, zero-sum choice between the values of liberty and community." 178.

Taylor notes that the Charter has become a rallying point for Canadians from diverse regions and backgrounds and is viewed by Canadians "not just as an additional bulwark of rights, but as part of the indispensable common ground on which all Canadians ought to stand. For many people, it has come in the space of a few years to define in part the Canadian political identity." 179.

....

178.   Robert C. Vipond, Liberty and Community, Albany: SUNY of New York Press, 1991, p. 192.
179.   Charles Taylor, 'Shared and Divergent Values', in Options for a New Canada, edited by Ronald L. Watts and Douglas M. Brown, Toronto: the University of Toronto Press, 1991, p. 60.

Taylor also observes that Canada is faced with irreconcilable differences in the way we view rights:

> "Now the new patriotism of the Charter has given an impetus to a philosophy of rights and of non-discrimination that is highly suspicious of collective goals. It can only countenance them if they are clearly subordinated to individual rights and to provisions of non-discrimination. But for those who take these goals seri ously, this subordination is unacceptable. The Charter and the promotion of the nation, as understood in their respective constituencies, are on a collision course. The reactions to Bill 178 and much of the Meech Lake debate were eloquent on this score." 180.

Quebec's use of section 33 to uphold its discriminatory sign law meant the ruling of the highest court in Canada - quashing the sign law - was overruled by a provincial government.

This served to lend a great deal of false and deceptive legitimacy to an otherwise unconstitutional violation of rights.

Of course, it also aided the cause of separatism.

....

180. Charles Taylor, 'Shared and Divergent Values', in Options for a New Canada, edited by Ronald L. Watts and Douglas M. Brown, Toronto: University of Toronto Press, 1991, p. 61.

Here after all was Quebec, a province, tossing aside a ruling from Canada's highest court as though it was nothing more than some intrusive and irrelevant rebuke from a minor foreign government.

It also poisoned goodwill in Canada towards Quebec. As Conrad Black notes: "To most English Canadians, Quebec has clamoured for bilingualism for decades; yet at the moment when some hundreds of thousands of English Canadians had responded by sending their children to French schools and support-ing official bilingualism, transcontinental French media and many other gestures that were, whatever their practical value, at the least an evidence of good-will, Quebec rendered the English language forcibly invisible. As bilingualism finally became reciprocal, Quebec, of all the provinces, became by some mea-sure the most hostile to bilingualism."   181.

Quebec also used section 33 in a way that is historically significant.
        By using the override to prop up its Bill 178 sign law, an otherwise unconstitutional violation of freedom of expression, Quebec poisoned the co-operative spirit of first ministers during the Meech Lake discussions.

In this light, the use of section 33 can be seen as a turning point in the collapse of the talks. It is entirely

....

181.   Conrad Black, 'Enough is Enough', in Canadian Politics 91/92, eds. G. S. Mahler and R. March, Guilford: 1991, p. 6.

possible that section 33's already bitter legacy will come to include the separation of Quebec, if indeed the Meech Lake Accord would have been enough to prevent separation.

Saskatchewan's use of the override was less controversial for two reasons: One, it preceded and did not overrule a Supreme Court judgement. Two, it was limited to back-to-work legislation for striking employees who were forced to accept a conciliator's proposed contract which was at least a modest improvement over their existing collective agreement.

Governments in Canada have been ordering employees offering "essential services" back to work for years.

Other than the ire of some prairie trade unionists, Saskatchewan's limited use of the override simply didn't capture the public imagination in the way

Quebec's sign law usage of the override did.

Nonetheless, Saskatchewan's pre-emptive use of the override and Quebec's earlier, pre-emptive blanket application of section 33 were each still disturbing in their own right as they each constituted a previously unanticipated use of the clause.

The lack of discussion and debate prior to this was also cause for concern as it violated the full debate and full disclosure of the specific rights affected. In particular, Quebec's blanket use of the override, affecting an array of provincial legislation, was a disrespectful application of a constitutional instrument and another example of the lack of distinction drawn by governments in Canada between mere statures and the theoretically more permanent constitutionally-entrenched rights.

The blanket use of the override also cut off at the knees anyone who might otherwise challenge the fairness of the override-protected legislation.

In his guarded defence of the override, Russell spelled out several added safeguards he wants put in place, including a double enactment provision, before and after an election and full debate and disclosure of affected rights.

But in the view of this writer, Russell's suggested safeguards are not enough.

Let me assert that if are to continue to be afflicted with section 33, let it be limited to the federal government only.

It is an obscenity that a provincial government - any provincial government - can overrule the highest courts in Canada.

In the Quebec sign law application of section 33, Quebec overruled two of the highest courts in Quebec plus the Supreme Court of Canada.

Apparently the unanimous decisions of all three superior courts were not enough to convince Quebec that its sign law was an unwarranted violation of the fundamental human right of freedom of expression and an unconscionable contravention of both the Quebec and Canadian charters of rights.

In most cases, legislatures, federal and provincial will maintain a strong degree of the legislative supremacy they now hold. Most laws pased by governments will not be challenged by the courts.

A few laws, seen by citizens as denying their rights, will be challenged and if the legislature can meet the reasonable, 'demonstrably justified' test of section 1 in the Charter, the legislation will still stand.

In my view, Section 1 is sufficient. If legislation cannot meet the very reasonable requirements of this judicial override, this said legislation does not deserve to stand.

Provincial use of the override has further disturbing implications: The ability of a province to overrule the highest court in the land undermines our unitary court system which until section 33 had provided some uniformity of law and unity to a divided country.

Now, Quebec can overrule the Supreme Court as though it were just a meddlesome pest, undermining respect for the legitimacy of the Canadian judicial process while allowing Quebec to cut another tie that binds it to Canada, continuing its trend towards incremental separation.

The immediate victims in Quebec's sign law usage of the override were innocent merchants whose only 'crime' was that wished to continue advertising their own private businesses in the English language as they had for generations.

Quebec's sign law ensured that they would be put to considerable expense in changing their signs to French only, a language many of their customers may have found confusing or incomprehensible, at a likely cost of business.

The indirect victims were all Canadians who saw in Quebec's use of section 33 another anti-Canadian move from quasi-separatists, a move which went against the spirit of having two official languages.

It is one thing for government to be tardy in providing language services, it is quite another to go out of your way to slap punitive legislation on people who have done nothing wrong.

Quebec's action also belied the reality that Canadians from coast to coast to coast are bound by a single common language, even in Quebec where English thrives as a second language.

Much has been made of the pressure Bourassa was under from a Quebec public eager to diminish English language rights.

But the size of an angry mob doesn't make its position justified.

For weak political leaders - such as Bourassa - section 33 has closed the reference case escape route and has made it more posible for injustice to prevail, for governments to toy with fundamental rights that are meant to be above the whims of politicians.

Perhaps the most disturbing aspect of section 33 is that it casts a false air of legitimacy over that which should truly be considered illegitimate.

Provinces need to be told when they've gone too far in infringing on rights. But section 33 tells them that they're never wrong. Even though a right or freedom may be compromised in a manner that is unjust and unfair, a given government can get away with this because section 33 allows the violation to stand - and cloaks it in an air of legitimacy.

Section 33 takes the otherwise unconstitutional and forcibly makes it constitutional. It bludgeons a square peg of inequity into the round hole of rights and allows the perpetuation of rights violations. For all of the reasons cited in this book, the Notwithstanding Clause must not stand.

BIBLIOGRAPHY

1.   Ajzenstat, Janet, 'A Social Charter Eh? Thanks, But No Thanks', Hamilton: McMaster University Political Science essay, 1994.

2.   Allaire, Jean, et. al., A Quebec Free To Choose: Report of the Constitution Committee of the Quebec Liberal Party, January 28, 1991.

3.   Banting, Keith, and Simeon, Richard, And No One Cheered. Federalism, Democracy and the Constitution Act, edited by Keith Banting and Richard Simeon, Toronto: Methuen Publications, 1983.

4.   Black, Conrad, 'Enough is Enough', in Canadian Politics 91/92, edited by Gregory S. Mahler and Roman R. March, Guilford, Connecticut: Dushkin Publishing Group, 1991.

5.   Brimelow, Peter, 'The Maple Leaf For Ever?', in Canadian Politics 91/92, edited by Gregory S. Mahler and Roman R. March, Guilford Connecticut: Dushkin Publishing, 1991.

6.   Belanger, Michel, and Campeau, Jean, et. al., Report of The Commission On The Political and Constitutional Future of Quebec, Sherbrooke: Bureau d'information a Montreal, Sherbrooke, March 1991.

7.   Bergeron, Gerard, 'Quebec in Isolation', from
And No One Cheered, edited by Keith Banting and
Richard Simeon, Toronto: 1983.

8.   Beck, J. M., The Shaping of Canadian Federalism: Central Authority or Provincial Right?
Toronto: The Copp Clark Publishing Company, 1971.

9.   Braide, Don, & Sharpe, Sidney, Breakup: Why
the West feels Left Out of Canada, Toronto: Key
Porter , 1990.

10.   Brodie, Janine, 'Tensions from Within: Region-
alism and Party Politics in Canada', from Party
Politics in Canada 6th Edition, edited by Hugh G.
Thorburn, Scarborough: Prentice-Hall Canada, 1991.

11.   Brown, George, excerpt from speech, in Parliamentary Debates on the Subject of the Confederation
of the British North American Provinces, 1865.

12.   Cairns, Alan C., 'The Politics of Constitutional
Conservatism', from And No One Cheered: Federal-
ism, Democracy and the Constitution Act, edited by
Keith Banting and Richard Simeon, Toronto: Methuen
Publications, 1983.

13.   Cairns, Alan C., Charter Versus Federalism. The
Dilemmas of Constitutional Reform, Montreal:
McGill-Queen's University Press, 1992.

14.   Cheffins, R. I., & Johnson, P. A., The Revised Canadian Constitution. Politics As Law, Toronto: McGraw-Hill Ryerson Limited, 1986.

15.   Constitution Act 1982, Part One, Canadian Charter of Rights and Freedoms, section 1.

16.   Constitution Act 1982, Part One, Canadian Charter of Rights and Freedoms, section 33.

17.   Francis, Douglas, et. all, Origins, Toronto: Holt, Rinehart and Winston, 1988.

18.   Greene, Ian, The Charter of Rights, Toronto: James Lorimer & Company,   Publishers, 1989.

19.   Gwyn, Richard, The Northern Magus: Pierre Trudeau and Canadians, Toronto: McClelland and Stewart, 1980.

20.   Heard, Andrew, Canadian Constitutional Conventions: The Marriage of Law and Politics, Toronto: Oxford University Press, 1991.

21.   Hudon, Raymond, 'Quebec, the Economy and the Constitution, in And No One Cheered, edited by Keith Banting and Richard Simeon, Toronto: Methuen Publications, 1983.

22.   Johnson, William, '50% and we're gone:' Bouchard myths again', in The Hamilton Spectator, March 10, 1994.

23.   Kennedy, W.P.M., Essays in Constitutional Law, London: Oxford University Press, 1934.

24.   Knopff, Rainer, and Morton, F. L., Charter Politics, Scarborough: Nelson Canada, 1992..

25.   Kuruvilla, Dr. P. K., 'Quebec's Action Was Wrong', from Policy Options, Vol. 10, No. 4, May 1989, Halifax: The Institute for Research on Public Policy.

26.   Macdonald, John A., excerpt of speech, in Parliamentary Debates on the Subject of the Confederation of the British North American Provinces, 1865.

27.   Manfredi, Christopher P., Judicial Power and the Charter, Toronto: McClelland & Stewart Inc., 1993.

28.   Meekison, J. Peter, 'The Amending Formula,' from Perspectives on Canadian Federalism, edited by R. D. Olling & M. W. Westmacott, Scarborough: Prentice Hall, 1988.

29.   Milne, David, 'Equality or Asymmetry: Why Choose?', in Options for a New Canada, edited by Ronald L. Watts and Douglas M. Brown, Toronto: University of Toronto Press, 1991

30.   Milne, David, The Canadian Constitution, Toronto: James Lorimer & Company Publishers, 1991.

31.   Monahan, Patrick, Meech Lake: The Inside Story, Toronto: University of Toronto Press, 1991.

32.   Monahan, Patrick, 'Politics and Constitutional Interpretation', from Crosscurrent, Contemporary Political Issues, edited by Mark Charlton and Paul Barker, Scarborough: Nelson Canada, 1991.

33.   Monahan, Patrick, Politics and the Constitution: The Charter, Federalism and the Supreme Court of Canada, Toronto: Carswell/Methuen, 1987.

34.   Morton, F. L., Law, Politics and Judicial Process in Canada, edited by F. L. Morton, Calgary: University of Calgary Press, 1992..

35.   Morton, F. L., Russell, Peter, and Whithey, Michael J., 'The First 100 Charter Decisions', in Law, Politics and the Judicial Process in Canada, edited by F.L. Morton, Calgary: University of Calgary Press, 1992.

36.   Mulroney, Brian, House of Commons Debates, April 6, 1989.

37.   Olling, R.D., and Westmacott, M. W., The Confederation Debate: The Constitution in Crisis, Toronto: Kendall/Hunt Publishing Co., 1980.

38.   Quebec v. Ford et al, Supreme Court of Canada. Judgement of Dec. 15, 1988, in Peter H. Russell, Rainer Knopff, Ted Morton, Federalism and The Charter, Ottawa: Carleton University Press, 1993.

39.   Romanow, Roy, Whyte, Whyte, John, and Leeson, Howard, Canada Notwithstanding., Agincourt: Carswell/Methuen, 1984.

40.   Reference Re Alberta Statutes, In the Supreme Court of Canada, (1938) 2 S.C.R. 100, in: Peter H. Russell, Rainer Knopf and Ted Morton, Federalism and The Charter, Ottawa: Carleton University Press, 1993.

41.   Reesor, Bayard, The Canadian Constitution in Historical Perspective, Prentice Hall Canada Inc., Scarborough: 1992.

42.   Reuber, Grant L., 'Federalism and Negative-Sum Games' from Confederation In Crisis, edited by Robert Young, Toronto: James Lorimer & Company, 1991.

43.   Richler, Mordecai, Oh Canada! Oh Quebec!, Requiem For a Divided Country, Toronto: Penguin Books, 1992.

44.   Russell, Peter, 'Bold Statescraft, Questionable Jurisprudence,' from And No One Cheered, edited by Keith Banting and Richard Simeon, Toronto: Methuen Publications, 1983.

45.   Russell, Peter, Constitutional Odyssey, Toronto: University of Toronto Press, 1993.

46.   Russell, Peter, 'Standing Up For Notwithstanding', in F. L. Morton, Law, Politics and the Judicial Process, Calgary: University of Calgary Press, 1992.

47.   Scott, F. R., 'Political Nationalism and Confederation,' Canadian Journal of Economics and Political Science, VIII , August, 1942.

48.   Simeon, Richard, 'Concluding Comments,' from Canadian Federalism: Meeting Global Economic Challenges?' edited by Douglas M. Brown and Murray G. Smith, Kingston: Queen's University, 1991.

49.   Smiley, Donald, The Canadian Political Nationality, Toronto: Methuen Publications, 1967.

50.   Smiley, Donald V., The Federal Condition In Canada, Toronto: McGrawHill Ryerson Ltd., 1987.

51.   Smith, Jennifer, 'The origins of judicial review in Canada', in Law, Politics and the Judicial Process in Canada, edited by F. L. Morton, Calgary, University of Calgary Press, 1992.

52.   Stevenson, Garth, 'Federalism and Intergovernmental Relations,' from Canadian Politics in the 1990s, Third Edition, edited by Michael S. Whittington and Glen Williams, Toronto: Nelson Canada, 1990.

53.   Stevenson, Garth Stevenson, Unfulfilled Union: Canadian Federalism and National Unity, Toronto: Gage Educational Publishing Company, 1989.

54.   Stanley, G., A Short History of The Canadian Constitution, Toronto: Ryerson Press, 1969.

55.   Taylor, Charles, 'Shared and Divergent Values', in Options for a New Canada, edited by Ronald L. Watts and Douglas M. Brown, Toronto: University of Toronto Press, 1991.

56.   The Task Force on Canadian Unity, A Future Together: Observations and Recommendations, Ottawa: Minister of Supply and Services, 1979.

57.   Trudeau, Pierre, Memoirs, Toronto: McClelland & Stewart, 1993.

58.   Trudeau, Pierre, 'The Poverty of Nationalist Thinking in Quebec', in Towards A Just Society, edited by Thomas S. Axworthy and Pierre Elliott Trudeau, Toronto: Penguin Books, 1992.

59.   Trudeau, Pierre, Towards A Just Society, Toronto: Penguin Books, 1992.

60.   Trudeau. Pierre, excerpt from a speech, House of Commons Debates, 32nd Parliament, First session, April 15, 1980.

61.   Vipond, Robert C., Liberty and Community: Canadian Federalism and the Failure of the Constitution, Albany: State U.   of New York Press, 1991.

62.   Wheare, K. C., Federal Government, London: Oxford University Press, 1946.

63.   Whitaker, Reg, 'The Overriding Right,' from Canadian Politics 91/92, edited by Gregory S. Mahler and Roman R. March, Guilford, Conn.: Dushkin Publishing, 1991.

64.   Whyte, John D., 'On Not Standing for Notwithstanding', from F. L. Morton, Law, Politics and the Judicial Process, Calgary: University of Calgary Press, 1992.

Manor House Publishing
(905) 648-2193

www.ingramcontent.com/pod-product-compliance
Lightning Source LLC
Chambersburg PA
CBHW021831020426
42334CB00014B/584